To John,
God Bless you
You are Special!
Austin Miles

# THE REAL RINGMASTER

# THE REAL RINGMASTER

by Austin Miles
with Grace Davis

New Leaf Press

**First Edition**

Some names have been changed to protect certain individuals' rights to privacy.



Library of Congress number: 80-83458

International Standard Book Number: 0-89221-079-6

# DEDICATION

This book is dedicated to:

Jack Anderson and Britt Hume, whose integrity saved my life, making this story possible.

My daughter Lori and my loving and patient wife Valerie, who lived with a clacking typewriter months on end as this was being written, without whose love and emotional support this story could not have been told.

# CONTENTS

## Part One

# Part Two

# 1
# A Guy and His Doll

The Westbury Music Fair was filled with an expectant audience for a performance of the musical *Guys and Dolls.* During intermission a beautiful ballerina made a hurried trip to the backstage pay phone. "Hi, Larry," Debbie said with enthusiasm. "Tell me, do you know Kokomo the Clown?"

"Sure, Deb, know him well. Kok's a good friend," he replied.

"I get such a kick out of his newspaper column," she said. "I'd love to meet him and see what he's like; maybe if you would introduce me to him, I could get us both some publicity."

"Sure, be glad to," Larry responded.

The first time "Larry" and I had met was in a line at the Steak Fare on Broadway. We had gotten into a conversation and eventually had become friends.

When Larry called me at 12:30 A.M., there was no hesitation on my part to saying yes to the breakfast invitation for the next morning, even though I knew the check would wind up in my hands.

Through the window of the tiny coffee shop in the Hotel Knickerbocker, I made out Larry's figure making its way through the usual New York sidewalk crowd. He made a grand entrance, stopped just inside with a sweeping gesture, and lifted both hands toward my table. "There's Kokomo!" his voice echoed from every corner of the room.

Patrons in the coffee shop, their faces expressionless, looked at him, toward me, back to him, then back to their plates of food.

"Why does he always have to make such a spectacle of himself?" I thought to myself uncomfortably. It took a few moments for me to realize that the graceful blonde standing behind him was his companion.

"Hi, pal," he said, squeezing my arm as he reached around to the girl. Taking her shoulders, he moved her forward toward me. "Say hello to Debbie, my ex-wife," he said in a tone that underlined his contempt for women. "We're all good friends."

I was studying her as he talked. She had bright blue luminous eyes; her nose had a slight hump, but not enough to detract from her beauty. Her mouth was a trifle on the small side. Slightly pronounced cheekbones molded her face in a classical Roman look. Her long neck and perfect posture gave her the grace of a swan. It was obvious that her mascara and pancake makeup had been left over from the night before. I overlooked it. "She must be the most beautiful girl I've ever met," I thought, as my hand slowly extended itself toward hers.

"Hello," she said, almost timidly, taking my hand in both of hers. "I'm glad to know you."

Her hands were warm. She fixed her eyes on me and held me in her gaze for a few seconds. Although she seemed in command of her femininity, I sensed an uneasiness about her. Her hands were trembling as she squeezed mine.

"Why should she be unsure of herself?" I wondered.

"What do you do, Debbie?" I asked, wanting to know more about her.

"I'm a dancer," she said, somewhat nervously. "I'm working at Westbury Music Fair right now. I'm auditioning this afternoon for *Paint Your Wagon.*"

"Deb's a great dancer," Larry broke in. "The best."

"I used to be a tap dancer," I said, "and I've never lost my feeling for it. I would love to see you work sometime."

"Why not come to Westbury and see the show?" Debbie asked enthusiastically. "We'll be there two more weeks." Again her eyes captured mine, holding them. I felt an urgency in her voice that indicated she really wanted to see me again.

"I'll try," I said. "I have some more writing to do, and

then the circus will be reopening, so I'll be on tour again."

After we had eaten, Larry glanced up and saw the waitress making out our check. "I gotta make a couple of phone calls from the lobby," he said in haste. "I'll join you both at the car." He made his timely escape just as the waitress put the check on the table. I picked up the check and held Debbie's chair as she rose to her feet.

"Well, what a pleasure it is to be with a gentleman," Debbie said, looking deeply into my eyes. "There are so few around these days. I just knew this was the way you would be." She seemed to have more control of her voice without Larry around.

After paying the check, I walked her across the street to the car. "Gee," she said, standing back for me to open the door for her, "let me enjoy this as much as I can."

"She really does seem to like me," I thought to myself happily. When she was seated, I gallantly closed the door. She rolled down the window, reached for my hand, and held it. Warmth and excitement flooded my body.

"You don't know how much I've enjoyed meeting you," she murmured. "More than you'll ever know." She seemed to be striving for the right words to say. Swiftly regaining her composure, she said with a steady voice, "Kokomo, you're the most fascinating man I have ever met."

Nobody had ever said such a thing to me. I was speechless as I felt her gently pull my hand toward her. Slowly I bent toward the window of the car. She kissed me in a way I had never been kissed before. It was like an electric shock!

"I must see you again," she pleaded. Her voice sounded sincere, almost desperate. "Please come with me to the theatre tonight, and we'll go out together afterwards."

"That will be great," I said with uncontainable joy in my heart. "Where shall we meet?"

"Penn Station at five o'clock. We'll take the train out."

"What about Larry?" I asked.

"Oh, there's nothing between us anymore. We're just friends."

Larry was coming out of the hotel. "See ya later, Kok," he said after he had climbed into the car. As the car drove away, Debbie turned to look back at me and smiled.

I felt a spring in my step as I walked lightly up Forty-fifth Street to Fifth Avenue. Never had New York looked more attractive. "Hello," I said to a man who glanced over at me while waiting for a light.

"Well, hello," the startled man replied.

Never had I looked forward to an evening with more anticipation. I could do nothing constructive for the rest of the day. Debbie had completely mesmerized me.

How much I needed someone special to fill the lonely void in my life! From the age of nine, when I had decided to go into show business, all my energies had been devoted to perfecting the skills of magic, juggling, dancing, and acting. There had been no time to develop personal, intimate relationships. After the completion of a successful tour with Spike Jones, I entered the world of the circus as Kokomo the Clown in a Broadway production called *The Littlest Circus.*

Rave reviews in the New York papers opened a variety of new doors, and my career spiraled steadily upwards. Even though I achieved "star" status and could hold the full attention of an audience from the stage, I was painfully aware of my inadequacies on a one-to-one basis. Lacking New York sophistication, I was a social bomb. Most of my offstage hours were spent in the lonely confines of my room.

It was there that my newspaper column, "The Tall and the Short of It," was born. Spawned from reflections of the many different people who had crossed my path, the column delved into a wide spectrum of human personalities from Eddie Carmel the Giant to Sonny Riley the Midget. And now it was responsible for my meeting this lovely girl. I was twenty-six at the time; the year was 1960.

We met at Penn Station at five o'clock and rode the train to Westbury. Somehow we managed to get seats. As our hands automatically met, I felt the tension in her again.

"Is something bothering you?" I asked with genuine concern.

"Oh, no," she answered. "I'm always a little nervous before a show at night."

While she dressed for the show, I sat on a stool in the

backstage area near the entrance ramp.

"Can I help you?" said a man, approaching me. He was the stage manager.

"I'm with Debbie," I said, pointing proudly.

"Oh, yeah," he replied with a strange grin. "O.K."

The house lights dimmed. The spotlight hit the music director as he entered and stepped up to the podium. He acknowledged the applause with a bow. Everything hushed as he lifted his baton in the air, hesitated a moment, then brought his hands down to start the lively overture of *Guys and Dolls.*

For a moment she sat down with me backstage. In her brief costume she looked stunning, sensuous, elegant. We held hands. As she rubbed my fingers ever so gently, I thought, "This must be the greatest day of my life."

As each number ended, she quickly changed to her next costume, then joined me again, talking to me and caressing my hand until the next number. I don't think I was ever happier.

Later, as the train rattled back toward Manhattan, in a rush of words Debbie said softly, "I don't want to ever be away from you. I need a home with a man I can really love and be a good wife to."

With total ecstasy flowing through my body, I held her in my arms. She pulled me to her tightly. The moments we shared that night were unlike any I had ever imagined possible. I never wanted this joyful love to end. The next day we set a wedding date. After all, when two people are so right for each other, why wait? I was wildly in love for the first time in my life.

Two weeks later Debbie and I were married.

Kokomo playing the drums in "The Littlest Circus."

Kokomo the Clown with "Little People," Jeff and June Dewsbury.

# 2
# The Clown Is the Fool

A drastic change came over Debbie after the wedding. She became flippant and argumentative. And although the marriage bed became a place of denial and hostility, I reasoned that her tours and demanding schedule as a dancer were putting her through a period of exhaustion.

I had booked a cruise where we were to combine our talents of magic and dancing for a paid honeymoon to the Caribbean. I thought optimistically that it would be a good rest for both of us.

On sailing day we stood and watched the passengers coming aboard. "Look at all those phonies!" Deb exploded, as she mimicked them with heavy sarcasm. "Not us; we're going to have FUN."

There was a first-night-at-sea costume get acquainted party. "I won't wear this stuff!" Debbie yelled, as she threw her costume across the stateroom.

I reacted with shock. "I don't understand, Deb," I said. "I thought you would enjoy it. People save up for years for a trip like this, and we're getting it free, even getting paid for it."

"I hate it," she screamed.

Slowly, I sat down in a chair. What was wrong? "What is it you want me to do, Debbie?" I asked her softly.

"I don't know," she said, sobbing hysterically. "I just know I'm not coming out of this stateroom. I'm staying in here for the whole cruise. If you really love me, you'll stay in here with me."

I put my hand to my forehead. How I had looked forward to this trip, hoping to spend every available moment up on deck breathing the fresh air, a luxury so lacking in New York City. She would have me cooped up in a stateroom for nineteen days?

Although Deb finally agreed to leave the room, the cruise turned out to be a disaster for me.

Debbie began to insult people on the trip, creating an atmosphere of hostility in which it was almost impossible to work. Her animosity was not confined to the cruise passengers but extended to the other artists, causing my relationships with them to suffer.

I was puzzled and angered. The cruises had meant a professional advance for me and a wonderful chance to get out of the city. For her they seemed merely to be an exasperating experience.

I was not surprised to receive a cablegram from the Abramson Booking Agency that all my future cruises with them had been cancelled.

After two months of marriage a black cloud of depression settled over me. Not only had Debbie become snappy in every conversation with me, but her appearance was becoming slovenly, and she was putting on weight.

Sitting in our tiny apartment in Manhattan, I finally broke the silence. "Debbie," I said slowly, "I know I don't have much to offer a girl, but I do love you. I honestly don't know what else I can do. Everything about me seems to irritate you. I'll never understand your behavior on that cruise ship, and I'll probably never be able to work a cruise again because of it."

Her lip began to quiver. She was about to break down and cry. She came over to the couch where I was sitting and put her arms around me, sobbing softly.

"What is it, Deb? Please tell me."

"Please . . . don't hate me," she began hesitantly, "but . . . I'm pregnant!"

"You're what?" I exclaimed.

"Yes, we're going to have a baby."

My heart quickened with delight. "Good grief, why didn't you tell me before?" I asked excitedly.

Her eyebrows arched, and her eyes opened wide as

though suddenly enlightened. "Because," she said, a smile appearing on her face, "I didn't think you would want one. So soon and all."

"Are you kidding? This is wonderful!" I exclaimed happily. "When?"

"I'm not sure," she said, wiping the tears from her face with a look of relief.

"I have another circus tour coming up," I said. "You shouldn't be left here; you should be with me so I can take care of you, except . . ." –I was thinking of her behavior on the ship. Debbie picked up on my thoughts.

"No, don't worry," she interrupted. "I'll be good. I wasn't feeling well on that ship. I was having morning sickness, and I was so nervous not knowing how you would feel about it. . . ." She was groping for words. "I was so afraid that when you found out, you wouldn't love me anymore—that you might leave me or something."

I reached out to her and pulled her to me. "Oh, Debbie, honey, if only you had known that nothing would have made me happier than to think that our love could produce a baby."

My wife of six months was having a bad day. The baby she was carrying was particularly active. Waves of nausea and pain engulfed her at frequent intervals. That night severe contractions started, and we rushed her to the hospital. In the waiting room of the maternity ward, I could hear her screams coming from the delivery room. They lasted all night. They began to sound more like screams of utter despair than of pain.

Finally, the next morning, the doctor came out and told me that Debbie had given birth to a full term baby girl. I followed a nurse to a glass window where the baby was held up for me to see.

Later, when I walked into my wife's room, she covered her face. It was wet with sweat and tears. She was sobbing quietly.

"Please forgive me," she begged between sobs.

"Who's the father," I asked.

"I don't know." She was now sobbing loudly, and I could see it was hurting her. She was still in pain from the difficult delivery. I turned away from her.

"Please, please forgive me. I really do love you. I'll spend the rest of my life making it up to you–honest I will," she cried.

She had had a rough time and had suffered terribly during that all night delivery. She looked so fragile and helpless that I reached for her hand.

"It's all right," my voice quivered softly, trying to adjust to the decision I was making.

"You won't divorce me?" she asked incredulously.

I shook my head no. We had only known each other for two weeks before we were married, but I had fallen head over heels in love with her. More tears were streaming down her face. She looked so delicate and beautiful that I was filled with compassion and gently bent down and took her up in my arms. Then I closed my eyes, trying to get used to this whole new situation.

# 3
# The Little Bitch

Soon after she returned home with the baby, Debbie became pregnant again. Her parents were outraged because the second pregnancy followed the first one so closely, making it impossible for her to resume her dancing career.

We took a hotel apartment on Broadway, in the heart of Manhattan. It was time for the Frank Wirth Circus to reopen at the Island Garden in West Hempstead, Long Island. I wanted her to come out that night to see the performance, but she declined, saying she wanted to rest and would come during the week.

How very much I wished Deb could have been there that night to have seen my performance. I couldn't wait to get home to tell her what had happened. The moment the performance ended, I grabbed a handful of change and headed for the nearest pay phone.

"Hi, sweetheart, it's me," I said excitedly.

"Wh-where are you?" she stammered. I detected nervousness in her voice.

"Here at the Garden," I bubbled over. "You'll never imagine what happened tonight! We had a new ringmaster, and you'll never guess who it was." I glanced down at the black boots and white breeches I was wearing, then at the lapels of the red tails.

"Well, I don't know," she hesitated.

"Come on . . . try," I urged.

"You?" she asked, making a wild guess.

"Yes, yes!" I exclaimed, thoroughly keyed up. "The regular ringmaster got sick. Actually, dead drunk is more like it. Frank Wirth caught me just before I got to the clowns' dressing room and asked if I could do it. Once I had told him I thought I could be a good ringmaster, so I said sure. I wore the other guy's suit. Look good in it, too."

I was talking faster and faster with fervency as the description allowed me to relive this memorable night.

"Wait a minute; slow down," she interrupted. "I can barely understand you. How did you do?"

"Excellent, without a flaw," I answered proudly. Everyone on the show said I was great. Not only that, there were two big booking agents in the audience, and they said they can keep me busy and at great money. It's a real break for us!"

"That's wonderful," Deb said, having regained her composure. "What time will you be home?" she asked softly.

"As soon as I get dressed and the bus and subway get me there," I replied with anticipation.

"Guess that means about an hour and a half?" she asked.

"That should be about right," I answered. "And by the way, I love you, Debbie."

"I love you, too," she said. "More than you'll ever know."

Kokomo the Clown was now a part of my past. My new role as a ringmaster was receiving great acclaim, not only from circus fans but from the press as well.

It seemed strange to look at the program and instead of seeing my name listed as a clown, to see my new top billing as *Ringmaster!*

I was doing a circus presentation at the St. George Theatre in Staten Island the day my wife's contractions began.

The manager of the show took care of the last introductions while someone sped me to the Staten Island Ferry to arrive just as it was ready to leave. Once across the river, I grabbed a cab and headed for the hospital.

I had a certificate with me showing I had gone through a course to learn how to assist in the delivery. In the hospital, with the red tails streaming out behind me, still wearing my top hat, I headed straight into the delivery room. Starting immediately, I applied hand pressure on Debbie's back with each contraction. It was only a half hour before I met my daughter, Lori. She was a mess! And she was mad!

Standing in that hospital wearing the full ringmaster's costume, holding my daughter whom I had helped deliver, I truly felt I was presenting "the greatest attraction on earth."

Several months later I came home to find Debbie sitting glumly in a chair holding the oldest daughter. Little Lori was lying alone in a chair across the room, Debbie glaring at her.

"What's wrong?" I asked nervously.

"I didn't want the little bitch to start with!" Debbie screamed, losing all restraint, her eyes fixed on Lori.

My mouth dropped open with shock.

"I did everything to get rid of that little bitch. I even went to the studio and did butterflies for three hours straight," she ranted.

In ballet, butterflies consist of flying, twirling, leaping splits. It's a violent movement that she had hoped would abort her pregnancy.

I stammered with unbelief, "But, honey, you said you wanted a family."

She screamed hysterically at the top of her voice, "I never did want another brat. I didn't . . . I didn't . . . I didn't . . . I DIDN'T!"

I was almost speechless. "I don't understand."

"I don't want that one," she raved. "Every time the nurses brought that little bitch to my room for their so-called mother-and-child get acquainted time, I got out of bed, went in the hall, and smoked until they took her back. I didn't even want to see the little bitch, let alone hold her, and I still feel the same way!"

After this outburst, she plopped down in a chair by herself. I walked slowly across the room and gently picked up my daughter. Lori had been born with a birth defect—crooked feet that turned inward. This condition never seemed to invoke much sympathy from her mother. On the contrary, the deformity seemed to be the root of Deb's violent rejection of the baby, since Debbie prided herself on her beautiful feet and dancing ability.

Little Lori was so tiny, she could be held with one hand. With my forefinger I felt the hair on the back of her neck.

It was so soft. Her little profile was mine in miniature. Little Lori then tilted her head, looked me in the face wide-eyed, with the corner of her mouth raised in a grin. I could no longer hold back my feelings. Holding her close to my heart, I broke down and wept.

# 4
# Telltale Teddybear

As word of my ability as a ringmaster began to spread, more and more offers for bookings came in. I accepted some traveling dates apprehensively. It was an opportunity to earn a lot of money, but I longed to be back in New York.

When the American Guild of Variety Artists started a new youth's program for the city of New York, it served a dual purpose for me. I could work in a constructive program and be near home.

Beginning with a performance in a school auditorium, the actors would return once a week for a specified period of time, teaching their crafts to the neighborhood youngsters. Comedian Joey Adams, who was then president of AGVA, spearheaded the idea. My job was to teach magic and juggling.

One day I returned home early, giving the downstairs buzzer a gentle beep that I was on my way up. As the elevator stopped at our floor, I heard the slam of a door. Approaching my apartment, I heard footsteps scurrying down the stairs. When I opened the door, there was my wife standing in a thin, brief negligee. She was trembling.

"How come you're undressed this time of day?" I asked puzzled.

"Come here," she said seductively, motioning me to the couch.

"Answer me, Deb," I said, fighting worry and suspicion.

"I just thought it was time we livened things up around here. I'm bored stiff. I'm losing my own identity. I can't stand being cooped up here with the kids. I'm going back to work," she retorted arrogantly.

"Do you intend to do another show?" I asked matter-of-factly.

"No, something else. I've been offered a position with a modeling agency. I'll be booking models."

Against my objections, she got a baby sitter and took the job.

It was then that her personality began to change. She was spending many of her evening hours with models with whom she had become friends, and I never knew at what hour she would be coming home. "Photography conference" would be the standard explanation.

Once a photography assignment came in for a young businessman type. "You might be right for this," she said, "but it wouldn't be good if anyone knew we were married. They would think I was favoring you." So for that one assignment, I signed in with the name Alan Squire.

The modeling agency appeared to be just what it advertized, an agency for photographers' models specializing in media ads, catalogs, and print work. The people who worked there, male and female, were beautiful people.

I resumed my circus work, traveling alone. Even though I was earning a great deal of money, I stayed in second-rate hotels to have more money to send home for the family. I was lonely and miserable.

I called home every night. Some nights there was no answer at all. When I returned home for the holiday break, I found the children were gone. Upon learning that they had been staying with Debbie's parents, I insisted we go and bring them back.

"Why are the children in New Jersey when we have a sitter in New York?" I asked.

There was a major row with my in-laws, but we returned to New York with the girls. On Christmas a big parcel arrived from them. In the package of presents for my wife and the two babies there was a vicious letter addressed to me.

When the time came for my next circus tour, I left reluctantly. I was worried about the hostility Debbie displayed toward Lori. It would have put me so much more at ease to have been able to take her with me. But then again, how could a man traveling alone take proper care of an infant on the road? I found myself saying, "Please, God, protect her."

Many of the circuses were sponsored by the Shriners. I had just arrived for one such circus in Louisiana. Following an early morning TV appearance to plug the show, I returned to the hotel. Nearly exhausted from the demanding schedule and the emotional worry of not knowing what was happening at home, I stretched out on the bed and quickly dropped off to sleep. The ringing telephone awakened me shortly after I dozed off. Irritated, I answered. It was long distance calling for Debbie.

"Operator," I asked, "what city is calling?"

"Washington, D.C.," came the reply. "Is Debbie there?"

"She is not here," I stated. "She never travels with me. She stays in New York. How did you know where I was staying?"

"Thank you," said the voice and hung up.

I stared at the phone. Even the circus producers didn't know the hotel in which I was staying.

Now that I was awake, there was no use trying to go back to sleep. Automatically I reached for the TV set as I started to dress. I froze in my tracks as the news bulletin announced that President John F. Kennedy had just been shot.

Quickly dressing, I headed for the circus arena. An "extra" edition of the newspapers was being delivered to the news vendors. "What's the latest on the shooting?" I asked.

"The President just died," the news vendor said, handing me the edition.

Backstage at the circus, all the performers had gathered. The Three Stooges were there, and all of us shook our heads in disbelief as we discussed the situation. "How the President affects people in every walk of life," I thought, looking over at this gathering of circus performers and the movie comedy trio. What a coincidence that phone call from Washington came just before the news of the asassination. It was puzzling.

Christmas back in New York with my family was not a happy time. My wife was constantly disagreeable. One afternoon, as the children were running across the floor, the phone rang; the woman who lived below us was calling to complain about the noise.

"Are you Catholic?" Debbie demanded.

"Why, yes," the woman answered.

"Good. Your church says we're all supposed to have babies and can't get rid of 'em, so you can live with the results, ya creep!" she declared indignantly, slamming the phone down.

Then my wife flew off into another rage, yelling, "I can't stand these kids, especially that little bitch!" She pointed at Lori.

Poor little Lori. I am sure for the first couple of years in her life, she thought her name was Little Bitch.

"One day when you were gone," she continued, "Lori broke loose from me in Central Park and headed for the roadway, and I sat for awhile, wondering whether or not to go get her."

I rocked with horror at the implication of this statement. I pictured that four lane road winding through the park and the wild way in which the cars sped through. Lori could well have toddled out on that busy roadway and been run down in an instant.

"Debbie, I'm convinced you are sick!" I yelled. It was a reaction of disgust and terror.

Suddenly she stopped her outburst and sat silently looking at me.

"You need help," I continued, more low-keyed. "This is not normal behavior."

"And what is normal?" Deb retorted, raising her voice again.

"Look, I don't mean this in a cruel way. But I think for your sake and all of ours, you should get therapy. Would you be willing to see a psychiatrist?"

I expected an additional outburst, but Debbie walked quietly over to me, sat down, put her head on my shoulder, and sobbed.

"There's a psychiatrist I used to know," she offered. "I'll call him and make an appointment."

I held her tenderly. How desperately I wanted to see her and our situation improve. As we sat, the oldest child toddled into the room, carrying her teddy bear. Reaching the center of the room, she stopped, put the teddy bear on the floor, and sat straddled on top of it.

Stunned, I watched silently. What little intimacy we had shared had been late at night behind closed doors, and nothing in our relationship resembled what the baby was imitating.

We both looked away, lost in our own thoughts.

# 5
# Gone

My wife began regular appointments with the psychiatrist, but to my disappointment there was no improvement. On the contrary, during her therapy she seemed to develop even more antagonism toward me.

One day, while she was at work in the modeling agency, the phone rang in our apartment. It was the doctor. "Could you come and see me at my office? I want to talk to you about your wife."

I readily agreed to see him, and an appointment was set for the following day. Most anxious for any insight into her behavior, and hoping to learn where I might be lacking in the relationship, I arrived with anticipation only to be asked the usual questions regarding my relationship with my father and my mother.

"Now this will help me to help you to help your wife," he said, sitting cross-legged on a hassock, puffing a pipe. He looked a little wild-eyed behind his glasses. He was wearing a sport shirt and slacks, bare feet protruding from sandals. There was nothing professional about him or his office. He seemed totally uninhibited to the point of being sloppy. Passed on the street, he would have appeared to be just another oddball. Yet, I concluded with my youthful naiveté, he must be imbued with special knowledge. After all, people did pay him twenty dollars an hour to straighten out their lives. "Looks sure can be deceiving," I thought, hesitating to trust my own opinion.

"I need to know something about your early sex experiences," he continued, taking down notes.

Desperate to be of any help possible, I spoke of my

early life with all candor and honesty. Trusting the doctor, my only thoughts about our conversations were that he would analyze the information for one purpose—to save our marriage.

When the time came to leave for my next circus tour, I felt unusual anxiety as I kissed Debbie goodby at the apartment door. Assuring me that everything would be all right, she said goodby again as I started for the elevator. "Wait, why not ride down with me?" I asked.

"O.K.," she suddenly decided. We walked together in silence to the sidewalk. While waiting for a cab, an actress-model friend of Debbie's who lived in the building was just coming home.

"Hi," she said, suppressing a giggle. "Hey, I've gotta tell you something about that last airplane ride. . . ."

The expression on Debbie's face tightened. Quickly the subject was changed. It was a peculiar reaction.

"See you later," the redheaded model said affectionately to Deb after noticing the curious look on my face.

Debbie's face relaxed again. The cab pulled over. From there I was driven to the airport, then flown down South for another circus tour.

The first letter I received from Deb on tour told me that Ron from the modeling agency had come by to help her paint the apartment. It was a cheerful letter, but it left me feeling uncomfortable, knowing another man had been in the house while I was gone. Yet, she had told me about it, and I couldn't allow myself to develop an attitude of jealousy or suspicion when there might be no real cause. After all, her desire to stay in psychiatric therapy must have meant she really wanted to straighten out our lives.

However, the letters following became more and more negative toward our marriage. My career as a ringmaster was advancing steadily, but my marriage was going down the drain.

Sitting with the music director of the circus and his wife in a seafood house in Gulfport, Mississippi, I felt the urge to call home. Excusing myself, I left the table, got a handful of change, and dialed my number.

"The marriage is over," Debbie said resolutely. "I've given it a lot of thought. It's never been good. The more I'm in analysis, the more I realize that it doesn't have a chance."

"Honey—please—I don't believe that. I'll cancel my tour and come home on the next flight."

"I wouldn't," she urged. "You'll need the money. Without any money, you'll have even more problems."

"Look," I fumbled, "this part of the tour only goes for two more weeks. Please don't do anything until I come home, and we can talk this out. How are the children?"

"They're back at my mother's."

My heart sank. I hadn't expected that.

"O.K.," I said half-heartedly, "Maybe it will be just as well for the time being so we can be completely alone to talk. I'll be home in just two weeks."

That must have been the longest two weeks I have ever spent. Following our performance in Jackson, Mississippi, I immediately grabbed a taxi to the airport. The moment we landed in New York, I rushed to the apartment, fairly well running across the sidewalk to the door and then into the elevator.

As I put the key in the lock, the door was opened for me.

"Oh, no!" My voice was a whisper as my eyes assessed the situation.

"It's no use," Debbie said. "It's over." Then she rose from the sofa and walked over to the window. "I took some furniture I needed, and the kids are with my parents. We can never make a go of things. . . . I'm too afraid of getting pregnant again."

"Oh, Lord," I pleaded, "you can use something, or I could use something—anything. We can work it out."

"No," she said resolutely. "The only way I can really be sure that we will have no more kids is to have an operation, and," she added coyly, "I could never go through with such a thing." She had set up the logical answer for a man desperate to keep the woman he loved.

"But, honey, they can perform such an operation on a man," I said.

"Would you be willing to do that for me?" she asked, still looking out the window.

". . . Sure," I assured her.

"You really do love me," she said flatly.

"Have I ever given you any doubt about that?" I questioned.

"That would be just great," she replied with enthusiasm. "I know a doctor on Park Avenue who can do it right away. I'll call him the first thing in the morning."

We stayed together that night. I respected what I thought were her fears.

We visited the doctor, who had insisted on speaking to both of us prior to the operation. We both had to sign a document stating this decision was entirely mutual before he would perform it.

Stretched out on the table after local anesthesia had been administered, the operation began. With the first snip of the scissors, the thought occurred to me that I would never be able to father another child.

"You must really love your wife to do this," the anesthetist said to me.

"Oh, yes," I said. There was another snip. "Very much."

After a two hour rest, I was slowly helped to my feet and walked out to the waiting room to meet my wife. We left and hailed a cab.

Arriving back at the apartment, my head started to swim dizzily. I sank into the couch. My wife went to the phone and dialed a number. "Hi, I'm ready. O.K." Then she hung up.

"So long, darling," she said, a smile appearing on her face.

"What do you mean, 'so long'?" I asked with shock.

"I told you a long time ago it was all over."

I started to get to my feet. The pain was so intense I flopped back down. "My God, Debbie," I exclaimed, "I just went through a vasectomy hoping our marriage would make it!"

"Too bad," she said flippantly. "Win some, lose some."

"But," I said, "this means I can never have children with anyone else!"

"Oh, poor thing," she said, mocking pity, patting my cheek. "Bye, darling." With a laugh, she headed for the door. A guy had pulled up downstairs to pick her up.

She was gone! I looked around the stripped apartment. Walking unsteadily, the fresh incisions and stitches hurting, I staggered into what had been the babies' room. I was literally drunk with the reality of what had happened. It was dark. I stumbled over a tiny rocking chair that had been left behind. A little bell attached to it tinkled as I fell to the floor and lay there for the rest of the night.

# 6
# The Diary

I felt nailed to the floor when the morning sun began to find its way through the windows. Stumbling into what had been our bedroom, I noticed a bureau had been left behind. It was the one Debbie had used.

I made my way over to it and slowly opened the middle drawer. There were some old sweaters inside. In a daze I started to pull them out. Under the last one I found something lying there in the bottom of the drawer. Realizing what I had discovered, I suddenly snapped back to my senses. How on earth could she have forgotten it? Almost in slow motion, I reached down and picked up her diary. Taking it to the living room, I sank down into the chair.

For the first time my wife's real life was revealed to me. It started innocently enough. While in her teens, a young man had come to call while her parents were not home. Watching TV in the living room, they had fallen asleep on the couch. When her parents returned and found them, they called her a little tramp and lambasted them with accusations. Later, when Deb left home to go on a dancing tour with the Rockettes, her parents said that she'd sleep with any man she met and was bound for hell! "So," she concluded, "since I am being accused of it anyway, I might as well go ahead and do it."

My heart sank as I flipped the pages. Affair after affair was explicitly recorded. I began to get physically sick. My stomach retched. My senses were reeling. Numbness settled into my limbs as all of her encounters were revealed.

Her life with Larry, her former husband, and the orgies in which she had participated were discussed in vivid detail.

There was a sordid account of a broom closet escapade during a Christmas party. I felt myself about to choke and had to stop for a moment to give my stomach time to settle down long enough to continue reading. She was getting to the part about her life with me.

"He's such a square," she wrote. "When I asked him once if he ever wanted to run around, he said, 'Why go anywhere else?' What a schnook."

Then came explicit details outlining all those personalities with whom she had had affairs during our marriage. Name after name. How and when. I learned she was with someone the night I had called from the circus to tell her so proudly that I had made my exciting debut as ringmaster, all of which was described laughingly. The footsteps I had heard running down the stairs when I found her in her negligee—that encounter had ended just in the nick of time!

I was consumed with utter despair as I read of her affair with her psychiatrist. The need for therapy had given her an excuse to resume their clandestine adventures on the psychiatrist's couch. Adding insult to injury, under the guise of doing his work, he had advised Debbie to dump me.

Many of the things described were so bizarre I was forced to stop reading again. Despairingly, I buried my head in my hands. Surely this was all a hideous nightmare! But, no, unfortunately, I was very much awake. What a fool I had been. I imagined the entire city had been laughing at me.

I sat glued to the chair for a couple of hours before I could turn the page to read further. It was well that I had rested before turning that page, for I do not believe any human being could possibly have been prepared for what I found there. What I had thought to be the major jolt turned out to be a mere warmup.

The next page began to describe the activities of the modeling agency, where she was the booker. What I read put me in a catatonic state of mind as the words in the diary—times, events, and dates—came into full focus.

"Oh, my God," I mumbled. Just about all of the sordid activities had taken place in the White House! Many high ranking military and political persons were named. Who, what, where, dates, times—all in meticulous chronological order.

"My Lord," exclaimed the attorney I had engaged as he read the diary in his office. The explicit details were all there. The modeling agency was the contact point for Washington. A twin engine Beechcraft plane from Marine Air Terminal would take the playgirls to the Capital. They usually had escorts with them for a front, but the escorts went elsewhere once the girls arrived at their destination. Sexual perversions, listing many famous names, were vividly described. My legal adviser got up from his desk and walked around to the front of it.

"What do you intend to do with this?" he questioned.

"Run off a copy here for you to keep," I said slowly. "I'll keep the original. She intends to divorce me. This will be my defense!"

He told me the diary was more than enough evidence for my defense. He also indicated that it was highly dangerous material. He even tore out a few pages to protect people he knew. There was enough evidence without them, he assured me.

As he walked around to the back of his desk, shaking his head, he said, "If you published this as a book, you'd make a fortune."

I walked back to my hotel apartment. The newspapers at the time were carrying headlines of the Profumo scandal in England. "This thing makes that look like a Sunday school picnic," I thought.

# 7
# Custody

Sitting in my apartment, the after shock fell heavily upon me; I have no doubt one could truly die of a broken heart. I knew I was heading toward a nervous breakdown. My soul was in sheer agony.

Making my way outside, I trudged wearily to Bellevue Hospital and into the psychiatric emergency room. I had to hold my stomach the emotional hurt was so bad. As others in the waiting room came into focus, I noticed a man with a crippled club foot. He had come in to see a doctor, but it was obvious that he was suffering from an emotional hurt. As he crumpled in the chair, the pain seen in his face seemed to come from the very depths of his being. He leaned forward, grimacing, as a thought apparently brought him even more pain. Then he straightened up again. A feeling of love and compassion for this battered soul stirred within me.

There was a black girl, screaming hysterically, who was brought in locked in a strait jacket. She had to be strapped to the chair. Her head was jerking in all directions as she flailed in agony, reliving some personal hurt. I began to feel guilty. There seemed to be others who were worse off than I. I shouldn't be taking up a doctor's time. Others seemed to need him more than I. How deep were their wounds!

I pondered the hopelessness of it all. Then quietly rising from my chair, I walked out the door. It was almost a tragic mistake for me to leave that hospital. Seeing people together on the sidewalks—talking, laughing, on their way somewhere —magnified my loneliness and heartbreak.

After I closed my apartment door behind me, the walls of that empty place seemed to share my agony. I still could not reconcile what I wanted my wife to be with what she really was. Maybe it was just that—it wasn't really her that I fell in love with, but a girl conjured up in my own mind, a fantasy, as one would fall in love with a work of art. So I could not really miss her, only the memory of a girl created in my own mind. And that girl never really existed in the first place. I took some comfort in my conclusions.

I looked out my window and clearly saw the Park Sheraton Hotel directly across from our apartment. The shades were up in one of the rooms, and all the lights were on. I could see a couple making love. The thought of my wife with someone else flashed through my mind and made me physically ill, my stomach rebelling at the memory. The next day I left for the Midwest for a visit with my parents to try to get myself back together.

Even though I was comfortably surrounded by trees, flowers, and fresh air, soon it was time to return to New York. There were many unfinished things to be settled.

I was utterly amazed at the contents in the petition for divorce that was served on me. What astonished me more than anything else was the lengthy testimony from the psychiatrist. He stated that he had been "treating" me when actually he had seen me only once, at his request, to discuss my wife. All of the confidential information I had given him was now revealed in its entirety along with his "analysis," which added to and perverted what had actually been told to him.

Among the charges against me by my wife were that I had insisted against her wishes on having a vasectomy.

There were other ridiculous testimonies against me by "sworn witnesses" whom I had never met at all. A substantial amount of alimony and child support were demanded.

Debbie's petition was answered with the diary! Her witnesses conveniently disappeared when it was learned such a diary had been kept and that it was in the hands of the defense.

After much legal battling by the lawyers, it was finally agreed that I should have custody of Lori, and Deb would keep the oldest child. She and her lawyer did not receive any of the financial benefits they had hoped to get.

# 8
# The 'Hustle'

It was good to be back on the road again. There seemed to be extra pleasure in putting on the red tails and top hat, waiting for cue, then, with a timpani roll, clicking the heels of my riding boots and making the grand entrance, with much fanfare, into the center ring. Nothing on earth can compare with the colorful intrigue of the circus world. It was a land of fantasy that impressed me from my very first encounter as a place of optimism, laughter, love, adventure, and strength of mind over matter.

As we wound our way across the United States, I watched every performance with the same enthusiastic intensity as any wide-eyed youngster seeing the circus for the first time, a fact that was noted in several newspapers.

I truly enjoyed announcing each attraction. The grand, flowery introductions, spiced with many descriptive adjectives, came easily to me. It wasn't necessary to fake that enthusiasm. I was a natural fan.

From time to time I took little Lori with me. Circus people are very family oriented, and there was no problem finding a baby sitter on the show. While on the road, Lori came down with German measles. After the doctor saw her, I left her in the room with one of the circus wives while I was in performance. When I returned, I found the entire ceiling of the motel room covered with brightly colored balloons. The word had quickly spread that Lori was sick, and people were slipping over to bring her something–the balloon man had just left. Lori's next visitor was Robert Baudy, the tiger trainer. Her eyes opened wide with delight. Cuddled in his arms was a snarling baby tiger cub.

Even with all these wonderful distractions, the back of my mind still harbored a nagging curiosity as to what was happening with my wife and the final divorce action. A backstage phone call in Hartford, Connecticut, from my mother satisfied that curiosity. "I have some good news for you," she said.

"Your wife got a change of venue from New York to Nevada, and she got the divorce decree there. Papers have arrived stating your marriage is dissolved, and you have been granted permanent custody of Lori."

I almost leaped for joy.

"There's something else," she said, some puzzlement in her voice. "I received a phone call, but whoever it was didn't clearly identify himself."

"Yes, go on," I urged.

"He said, 'It's all over now. Just keep quiet about everything and forget it all happened.' It sounded like he was threatening."

"Don't worry, mom, it was probably just a lawyer," I said reassuringly. "Thanks for calling. This is great news." I hung up the phone. "Free at last," I mumbled. "Thank God. Now I can get that memory wiped out forever."

The opening night of a circus is always a hectic affair. We never believe we'll make it through the first show without artistic disaster. It is always such an ordeal that at the moment any other job in the world seems more appealing.

Following the first half of a particularly difficult opening show, I closed my dressing room door behind me and leaned against it for a moment, taking a long breath. I removed my top hat, wiped some sweat from my forehead, and responded to a gentle knock on the door. It was Bobby Yerkes, the catcher for the flying trapeze act. Bobby gave the impression of being a man who had known life's frustrations and disappointments but had managed to find a peace within himself and an ability to deal with the world around him. He had a Bible in his hand.

"I'd like to talk with you when you have a moment," he said.

"What about?" I asked.

"About your salvation," he replied with sincerity.

"Good God," I thought, "don't tell me we've got a religious nut right here in the circus!"

"I'd be happy to talk with you," I replied, "but my immediate salvation lies in my being able to get this show over with."

During the second half of the circus, I paid especially close attention to Bobby's act, studying him. He was an excellent performer. His flying trapeze act was the best in the business. I had to respect him for that, and it was to this aspect of him that I responded.

After the show he talked with me further. He wasn't condemning at all. Instead, he exhibited great warmth toward me, as though he really cared for me as an individual. Accepting some Christian literature he offered me, I agreed to go to the Christian businessmen's breakfast the next morning.

"How anybody could ever talk me into getting up at this hour, I'll never know," I grumbled after the hotel operator had called my room to cheerfully give me the glad tidings that it was 7:30 A.M.

At the breakfast Bobby introduced himself and me, saying that we were with the Shrine Circus. The men became obviously uncomfortable. They made a special point of TRYING to be nice to us and trying to welcome us. This disturbed me. If someone is truly welcome, it isn't necessary to fake it.

The chairman stood up to pray for the Lord's blessing upon the meal and the meeting. His voice seemed to quiver nervously, ". . . And we especially ask Your blessing upon our two special guests this morning, and the group they're with that is so difficult to reach. . . ."

My blood began to boil. I couldn't hear the rest of the prayer. Such prejudice. "How dare he?" I thought.

When the long monologue had ended, I doubt anyone heard me say, "Go to hell," as I left.

Bobby had also been upset by that prayer but stayed for the meeting as a courtesy. He tried to convince me that all Christians were not like that. "Besides," he said patiently, "the Bible tells us to keep our eyes upon God, not man."

"Such blind judging of people they know nothing about!" I said angrily. "If that's what being a Christian makes a person become, then I don't want anything to do with it."

It was only my high regard for Bobby as a person that caused me to yield and go to another Christian meeting.

"I know the men personally in this chapter," he said. "They're what Christians are supposed to be. I promise you, you will like them, and they will like you!" That last statement carried weight.

The members of that chapter were exactly what Bobby had promised, and I felt great rapport with them. In spite of the barriers I had put up, I was greatly enjoying their fellowship.

Their speaker was from New York.

When I was introduced as the special guest, his eyes lit up, and following his testimony, he headed straight toward me and shook my hand.

"I feel led of the Lord to pray a special prayer for you," he said. While I tried to resist, he clasped his hands on my head and gave a long prayer. "Didn't that feel good?" he asked at the end, trying to get me to agree. "Couldn't you just feel the presence of the Holy Spirit?" Then, before I knew what was happening, he was hitting me up for a big donation for his "vital work" in New York. It was hard sell.

"D–!" I thought. "That's all religion is, just one big money-making racket!"

Bobby Yerkes was absolutely crushed. He came to my dressing room before the show the next day. "Please don't let what happened turn you off; that would be tragic. That guy had no right to hustle you for money like that. The whole chapter was upset by it and will never have him back again. . . ."

"Bobby–please say no more about it," I said, staring him directly in the eye. "I like you and all that. You're great to work with. In fact, I wish every performer was like you. I enjoy your company. But you're not to ever, I mean EVER, try to sell me religion again. You know as well as I do that it's all a lot of crap."

"No!" Bobby interrupted.

"Please, Bobby, let me finish. I just want it understood that you are never to bring the subject up to me again."

"Sure, pal," he said, unable to conceal the hurt in his face. "I'll respect your wishes. I'll not bring it up to you again unless you tell me you want to discuss it. We'll still be friends." We shook hands and prepared to begin the show.

Bobby kept his word and did not bring up the subject again. He continued to extend his friendship to me. When the tour had ended, his eyes were downcast as we said good-by. Down deep, I sensed he felt he had failed me AND failed God. He seemed to feel a challenge to his own faith by that series of unfortunate events.

Neither of us could realize at the time that the stage was being set by a Divine director who was preparing to move in my life in a mighty way.

# 9

# Raised from the Dead

It was a clear fall day, and I was full of new found self-confidence as I sped toward Memphis. My circus tours had been going well, and I had finally indulged myself by purchasing a new car. In the past I had traveled by plane, but now I had a wonderful sense of independence in having my own transportation.

My recovery from the collapse of my marriage was going well. I had ceased to be so introspective and was socializing more with others. My daughter was safe in the hands of my mother in Evansville, and all seemed reasonably right with the world.

As I pulled into the grounds of the Mid-South Fair, workmen were busy putting up the carnival and food stands. I made my way into the main tent where the men were setting up the seats. A teterboard group was running through its act.

Gil Gray, the producer, was standing there, his white hair blown in all directions by the warm southern breeze. Gil, the master showman, wore a big diamond ring, with a diamond stickpin in his tie. His face was friendly but strong, gently creased with wrinkles. The ever-present cigarette in his hand was like a sixth finger. He greeted me warmly. We had never met but recognized each other from our photographs. Gil had his own small circus, which played the Western United States under the auspices of the Shriners. It was not one of the large circuses, but it had a reputation for elegance and excellence. It was known as "The Show Beautiful."

This would be a first-time thing for me, performing under a canvas tent. All my previous performances had been in arenas or ball parks. The tent was gorgeous. It was brightly colored and had purple velvet drapes at the performers' entrance. Above the entrance the bandstands were decorated with lamps. The ropes were spotlessly white, and the riggings were freshly painted. It looked like a Hollywood set.

A large crowd poured in for our opening night performance. Everything was running smoothly. Suddenly, in the middle of the show, there was a disturbance in the bleachers.

Normally a ringmaster tries to keep the regular routine going no matter what happens. Somehow this situation seemed different. I signaled to the band to stop playing. It was the first time I had ever stopped a performance. "What is it?" I shouted to the section of the bleachers where the disturbance seemed to be.

Someone shouted back, "Heart attack! Get a doctor!"

"Ladies and Gentlemen," I said into the microphone, "please keep your seats. I want all entrances kept open. Every second may be important in this man's life." I dispatched someone to go to the tower and radio for an ambulance.

Then I asked, "Is there a doctor or a nurse in the audience?"

A nurse identified herself and made her way over to the victim. She felt his pulse and listened for a heartbeat. She looked at me and shook her head. Someone tried chest massage. The nurse tried again for a pulse or heartbeat. Two or three men tried chest massage together, apparently thinking that more force might stimulate the heart to work.

A sense of gloom began to settle over the tent. I could feel the crowd beginning to get uneasy. It was so quiet you could hear the sounds from the free attractions outside.

In a sudden act of pure showmanship to keep the people in their seats, I extended my arm. Making a sweeping gesture that encompassed the tent, I said, "Will everyone here who has faith, in your own words and in your own way, bow your heads and pray earnestly for this man."

People in the audience began to bow their heads. Things became very quiet. I was unsettled by the sensation of a tingling going through my body. It was as if some power had entered the tent. After a few minutes I saw, out of the corner of my eye, ambulance attendants bringing in a stretcher. The man was placed on it and taken out.

"Amen," I said into the microphone. I moved quickly into the announcement for the next act. It was wire-walker, Veno Berosini. I could see in his face that he was extremely upset. Circus people have a tendency to be superstitious, and this certainly looked like a bad omen. We obviously didn't need an unsteady wire-walker that night. I signaled Veno that I was cutting his act and began to mentally reprogram the remaining routines. Talking to fill time, I looked over to Ruby Landrus, the dwarf clown from England. Ruby took my cue and came waddling over for some ad lib clown numbers with me. The audience needed some comic relief. They began to laugh and then to applaud.

We got the show back on the track. At last we brought it to a close with the finale, "There's No Business Like Show Business." All the performers came out in their capes and oriental costumes for the final spectacle.

When the arena was finally clear, I climbed into my car and headed for a quiet late dinner before returning to my motel. Sitting alone over my dinner, I mused about the variety of my circus experiences—the night an aerialist fell and I managed to catch her; fortunately the ceiling was lower than usual, so she was not at her regular height. We were both bruised, and my costume was torn, but it saved her serious injury, possibly her life.

Once we had an elephant stampede; another time I split the seat of my pants during a bow; and now, a heart attack in the bleachers. (There really is no business like show business.)

The next afternoon I arrived for the matinee performance. The previous evening's excitement was all a part of the past now. However, something was different. For one thing, everyone I passed seemed to have a greeting for me. Even the fellows in the radio-television booth called out a hello.

People didn't act like the typical circus crowd. Something definitely was in the air.

Little Ruby Landrus rushed up to me. "Where have you been? We've been looking all over for you," she said breathlessly.

"This is the time I usually arrive for the matinee," I answered, somewhat puzzled by her inquiry.

"Boy," she said, "that was really somethin' last night, wasn't it?"

"Yes, it was," I answered. "Any news on how the man is?"

"You mean you don't know what happened last night? The whole fairgrounds is talkin' about it!"

I looked at her dumbfounded.

"Well," she continued, with her heavily English-accented voice, "that man's heart had stopped beating–dead ya know! Things were very serious indeed! Then you did a wonderful thing. You asked everybody to pray."

I felt a growing sense of guilt. I was apparently being given credit for religious faith because of a show business gesture designed to keep the audience in the stands.

"I was standing right next to the chap," Ruby continued. "I bowed me head, too, but I kept one eye on him at all times! And then I felt a strange power sweep through the tent, and then the man started to breathe again."

"What?" I asked cautiously. "And today?"

"Today he's completely recovered. I'm not kiddin' ya! Ask anyone who was there. Even Mr. Young, the head of the fair, is talkin' about it. Anyway, I can tell ya somethin'; I'll be in church Sunday mornin'!"

For the rest of the day my mind was in a swirl of bewilderment, guilt, and anxiety. Had God honored my gesture of calling for prayer? Why? And WHAT was the power so many of us felt?

I was always ravenously hungry after a show, but that night I didn't want anything to eat. I got into my car and headed straight for the motel. I took out all the literature Bobby Yerkes had given me in our days together and read it. I looked at the desk. There was a Gideon Bible. For years I had been putting Gideon Bibles back in the drawer or placing things on top of them. Now something drew me to this one. I opened it at random. My eye fell on James 5:15, "And the prayer of faith shall save the sick, and the Lord shall raise him up. . . ."

The Bible had always seemed to me to be a complicated book full of "begats," names no one could pronounce, and wars in which no one was interested. But suddenly there was simplicity in the words I was reading. I pondered them for a few minutes and flipped the pages to see what else this book had to say. This time it fell open to St. Matthew 18:20, "For where two or three are gathered together in my name, there am I in the midst of them."

I began to think about the meaning of all that. We were in Memphis, part of what H. L. Mencken had described as the "Bible belt." There was a church on every corner. No doubt more than two or three believers had been in that circus tent agreeing on the healing of the victim, and their faith had turned a canvas tent into a cathedral!

Was I, I wondered, the only person in the tent who didn't have faith? I knew that Ruby Landrus had faith and that there were others in the circus who quietly read their Bibles. I, who had called them to prayer, must be one of the few who didn't have faith.

I had many spiritual questions and decided to fly to California to see Bobby Yerkes, who so often had tried to tell me about Jesus.

When he picked me up at the airport, I related to him some of the recent developments in my life, including the miracle under the big top. As I told him about that episode, the enormity of it grew.

"You're just in time," he said. "We're having a fellowship luncheon in Hollywood." There was no hesitation about my going this time.

There was something different about the men at this luncheon. As they prayed before lunch, I felt that same tingling go through my body that I had felt in Memphis when a man was raised from the dead.

Leaning over to Bobby, I said, "Bob, I felt something go through my body." The sensation moved me deeply. "Would you help me to pray?"

"I sure would, brother," he responded with enthusiasm as he took my hand and quietly led me in the "sinner's prayer."

# 10
# The Swiss Miss

My spiritual hunger had been partly satisfied, but I was still lonely. I knew that a broken marriage in the background would be a strike against me; however, I still hoped to find that special someone with whom to share my life.

While I enjoyed many friendships, I was convinced that most girls just played games and were not truly sincere.

Our current tour wound up in New York. Christmas trees and decorations were up as I was making plans to return to the Midwest for a visit with my mother and Lori. Hailing a taxi, I headed for New York's East Side Terminal.

It was a busy time of day. All of the airline counters had long lines of people waiting. I chose one being served by a tall, attractive brunette. As the line moved slowly forward, I had a chance to observe the young lady. She was a slim, nicely proportioned, good looking girl who exuded an elegant charm.

Approaching the counter, I heard a lovely Swiss accent. As her eyes glanced up with sudden interest, I captured her studious appraisal, then returned it. There was a natural loveliness about her, none of the make-up gimmicks. Her pleasant European face fascinated me. It was several seconds before either of us spoke.

"Are you traveling alone?" she finally asked.

"Yes," I responded.

She looked over at the hatbox I was carrying. "Do you have a wife?" she asked in her lilting Swiss voice.

"No, I don't have a wife," I said almost triumphantly.

"Then, why would a man be carrying a hatbox like that?" she asked curiously.

"Oh that! I'm a professional circus ringmaster, and this is the top hat I wear. I've just come off a tour."

My explanation seemed to delight her. "Oh," she said with renewed interest, "when I was a little girl, I used to go to the Circus Knie in Switzerland. I loved the horses. They were so beautiful."

As we continued in our absorption with each other, the people behind me began to move to the other lines with unidentifiable mumbling.

I told her I had been married and was on my way to spend the holidays with my daughter. She seemed fascinated by that bit of information.

"Well," she exclaimed, "I always wanted to meet a man with a little girl." She made no effort to suppress her interest. I suggested that I take her to dinner when I returned to New York after New Year's Day so we could talk and get acquainted.

We exchanged addresses and telephone numbers, and I learned her name was Rose Marie.

The encounter apparently rattled both of us—she sent my bags to the wrong city, and I tried to board the wrong plane.

It was always a happy occasion to be back in Indiana to visit my folks and Lori. Life was considerably less hectic in the country than in New York. I had given up my New York apartment and all its memories; yet I was constantly lured by the excitement of the city. New York seemed to me to be the heartbeat of the whole world. I loved the arts and culture available there. I was always being pulled between the desires for Midwestern peace and the frantic pace of New York, although I couldn't seem to get permanently attached to either place.

The newspapers and television carried stories of the subway and bus strike in New York, and that seemed to settle things for the moment. New York was an unmanageable place without public transportation. I did have one piece of unfinished business. Fishing out the card with Rose Marie's name on it, I dropped her a note saying, "Will see you shortly after the transportation strike is over." After that, I didn't give the matter much thought.

The transportation strike was finally settled. And the very next day a telegram arrived. It said, "When is shortly?" It was signed "Rose Marie."

I began to think about this lovely Swiss girl. Perhaps, I tried reasoning, the trouble lies with American girls. Perhaps European girls have a different perspective.

The telegram ended my ponderings about the possibility of staying in the Midwest. I notified her of the flight that would be bringing me to New York. She took the day off from work and made great preparations for my arrival.

We had a whirlwind courtship. She didn't speak of her family, and I didn't ask. Since they were across the ocean, I felt they were not important to our relationship.

We were married quietly by a justice of the peace in Reading, Massachusetts, in 1966.

When the day was over, Rose Marie seemed tense and jumpy. She spent most of the night lying on her back staring sadly at the ceiling.

"What is it, Rose Marie?" I finally asked her. "What's wrong?"

"It's just that . . . I don't know how to tell Uncle Fritz and the family."

Her apprehension was short-lived. Somehow, news of our wedding reached Rose Marie's uncle, who had acted as her stepfather in Switzerland. We had no sooner settled into our new apartment in Forest Hills, New York, when Fritz flew to America in a rage. As we were sitting in our living room one evening, someone shouting in German began to bang on the door.

"Oh, my God!" exclaimed Rose Marie, jumping to her feet. "It's my Uncle Fritz!"

I was puzzled. We were honorably married. We had no reason to fear her uncle or anyone else.

"Rose Marie," he shouted in broken English, "let me in."

Rose Marie, a grown woman of thirty-three, was rigid with fright. It did not make sense.

I opened the door. "Wie gehts, Herr Fritz," I said in a couple of the few German words I knew. It was a proper greeting.

Fritz Stitzel turned out to be a very wealthy retired Swiss banker who was suspicious of my motives for marrying Rose Marie. Eventually we agreed our discussion could be conducted more satisfactorily at the home of a Swiss friend of his, who was the head of a large pharmaceutical company in New Jersey, and who spoke fluent English. We joined him there the next day.

I was confused by the entire situation. The sum of Herr Stitzel's complaint seemed to be that I had married Rose Marie without proper clearance from him. It would be necessary, I was informed, for me to be investigated. As a first step, he handed me some sort of form. It called for a variety of information: parents' names, place of birth, amount of income tax paid in the previous years, and other personal data.

I threw the paper down in indignation. "I'm not asking you for a loan! I'm not asking you for anything! This is an insult!"

"Then I have come here for nothing," he stormed. "I know nothing about you."

"Let's get something straight," I said firmly. "I married Rose Marie for love. I had no idea your family had money. I thought Rose was just a European working girl."

"I just want it agreed," he said, assessing me, "that the Swiss francs remain in Switzerland."

That was the final straw. "Sir," I said with growing hostility, "you may take your Swiss francs and stuff them."

I stormed outside to the backyard, slamming the door. Rose Marie came out behind me. She was near tears.

Suddenly, Fritz's friend yelled out the window, "Come quick! Fritz is sick!" We rushed in. Fritz lay on the floor, clutching his heart.

Rose Marie sat on the steps, staring coldly down at her uncle on the floor. No emotion showed in her face.

The ambulance had already been called, but Fritz was beginning to turn blue. I could no longer stand idly by. I remembered that the man in the circus tent had been given chest massage. Going to him, I felt for his pulse. It was dangerously faint. Ripping his shirt off, I began to massage and pound his chest until the ambulance finally arrived.

"How long have you been doing this?" one of the attendants asked as he took over.

"About twenty minutes," I answered.

"You probably saved his life."

As they placed the oxygen mask over his face, Fritz took my hand, looked up at me, and said, "Danke (thanks)." The ambulance sped him off to the hospital.

The next day Herr Stitzel insisted on signing out of the hospital and returning immediately to Switzerland.

A short time later Rose Marie asked me to bring Lori to live with us in New York. I resisted for several reasons. I had promised myself that Lori would have a loving home and not be uprooted again. Since Rose had insisted upon keeping her job, I was still somewhat apprehensive. The money she made did not mean that much, but it was a symbol of her independence which she valued. I needed to be certain that this marriage was secure before bringing Lori to be with us in New York.

When Rose made a trip to Europe for rest and relaxation, she returned with a little red outfit for Lori.

We began to spend more time together, going to concerts and the theater and taking long walks. Soon it felt right to complete our family, so I flew back to Indiana, picked up Lori, and brought her home with me to New York.

Then we received an invitation for all three of us to come to Switzerland to be presented to the rest of the family. The fact that I was a circus performer caused Rose Marie great consternation. Apparently, Swiss banking families did not approve of circus people.

"How am I going to explain the fact that you're not with Ringling Brothers?" she asked nervously. "At least they would know about the Ringling circus."

Patiently I reminded her that the Shrine circuses were very big in the United States and that I made more money and had more independence with the Tom Packs Circus than I would with Ringling.

Arriving at what she thought was the best solution, she said, "We'll tell everyone you're the director of the circus."

"No!" I said defiantly. "I'm not a director. I'm recognized as America's top ringmaster. To me that's an accomplishment. I'm proud of my position, and I don't have to fake anything."

Zurich, Switzerland, lay sprawled out below us. Pointing out the plane window, Rose explained, "We are flying directly between the lakes for our approach. Isn't it beautiful?"

The German-Swiss architecture below, with the snow-capped Swiss Alps framing it, painted a picture that no artist could really capture on canvas.

When I saw the homes of the members of her family, I realized that the word *wealthy* was inadequate to describe their affluence. The homes were palatial. Inside, the walls were hung with tapestries, and the rooms were decorated with statuary. They looked more like museums than places where people actually lived. One had its own aviary. Original Rembrandts were commonplace. Their mode of transportation was the chauffeured Mercedes Benz. Strangely, Uncle Fritz Stitzel, who was the wealthiest of all, lived in an apartment and drove his own Mercedes.

We met with about thirty-five members of her family in an elegant banquet establishment. I was introduced to them, one by one, as they entered. I used all my memory skills from the circus to fix each name and title with each face. The family was Swiss-German and had the German reverence for titles.

As was the custom, I was supposed to acknowledge each member of the family individually, and when the time came, I was ready. I knew that the entire family had placed me under severe scrutiny. With great determination and definite preplanning, I intended to knock them on their aristocratic ears.

I was introduced to the family and rose to speak. "Herr Stitzel," I said, acknowledging the head of the clan with proper decorum and a bow, "and members of the family. Thank you so very much for your hospitality in greeting and welcoming us. The Swiss clock you gave us will always be a treasured possession in our home." Now I was building up to the finale.

"My parents in America extend their warmest greetings to all of you," I continued. "In fact, if they were here, they would say, 'Wie gehts, Herr Fritz Stitzel . . . Frau Rosilee Stitzel . . . Herr Doctor Deesay. . . .' " To their increasing astonishment, I pointed to each one, calling the correct name and title of every member of the family.

That broke the ice. I had disarmed them. They gave me a resounding burst of applause, which I acknowledged with a formal bow and then sat down.

"That really did it," Rose said as we walked around the Zurich lake. "They have to have respect for you after that."

Rose Marie was now determined to make an aristocrat out of me. During the next several months she trotted me through museums and concert halls in an effort to give me some "culture." We visited several countries on our cultural tour while she made an observation concerning my lack of formal education.

"If you had the right parents, you could have made something of yourself."

"I don't think I've done too badly," I countered defensively. "I'm considered the best in my field."

"Do you mean you intend to stay in the circus the rest of your life?" she asked.

"Why not? It's a great job, and I love it."

One day I came home, and my entire wardrobe was gone. "I threw it all down the incinerator," she informed me. "It's time you dressed with class."

"Rose Marie," I protested, "one of the first things you told me after we met was that you liked how well I dressed!"

"Well, it can be better," she said flatly.

"My sneakers?" I asked with apprehension.

"Yes, I threw them out, too. You are getting a whole new wardrobe."

"Oh, no," I groaned, "not my sneakers."

With the combination of my constant trips with the circus and Rose Marie's having her own job, we never seemed to have a chance to learn about each other. In a rare moment when she was able to talk about herself and her past freely, she explained her family situation and her relationship with Uncle Fritz.

Her father was an outstanding painter and restorer of cathedral frescoes. He had restored much of Michelangelo's work. Fritz Stitzel was married to her father's sister. When Rose Marie was four years old, her mother had become seriously ill and died.

Uncle Fritz and his wife took Rose Marie into their home and raised her as their own daughter.

"Uncle Fritz" was a man of extremes. He could run playfully down the mountainside with Lori, every inch the doting grandfather, and then fly into a murderous rage over a triviality. He totally dominated his family and expected its members to bow to his judgment. He had already picked out what he considered a proper husband for Rose Marie without consulting her.

Fritz had provided Rose Marie with a formal education, including finishing school in London. She was highly intelligent and fluent in four languages. He instilled in her his own hardeyed business sense, and a desire to be independent.

Rose had worked in a variety of positions, one of which was as governess for the children of the Italian ambassador, and another, as a stewardess for Swissair.

Leaving Europe to come to America to work was her most definite statement of independence. Marrying me had been another.

Yet she constantly worried about the possible loss of family inheritance. Every time a letter bordered in black arrived from Switzerland, she would open it anxiously. She then would wait with impatience for the next news—the will. When the first two family members disinherited her, she was crushed. "It's because I married you," she exclaimed, crying.

Finally, I could take it no more. "I wish they would all disinherit you right now, so you would depend on ME."

Another black-bordered letter arrived. At first she read with interest; then she broke down, weeping angrily. "That no good b—!" she screamed. She dropped the letter, which fluttered to the floor as she ran into the bathroom.

I picked it up and read it. Her father had died and left what valuables he had to an eighteen-year-old mistress.

# 11
# A Way Out

Rose Marie and I grew further and further apart. She no longer talked to me—she talked at me. Our marriage, although new, was already shaky, and our long separations did not help an already precarious situation.

When my first wife heard about my marriage, she was boiling mad. She began to hatch a vindictive scheme, with no thought of the serious consequences to all involved. Lori was the perfect pawn.

Rose Marie became hysterical when the papers were served announcing that a new custody suit was instituted. She had been caring for Lori for over a year and had grown quite attached to her.

Hysteria had begun in other places as well, since it was logical to assume I would use the diary again as my defense, and this time it was probable the newspapers would cover the proceedings.

By now the original diary had been given to a trusted friend for safe keeping. I received word from other friends in various circuses that FBI agents had been asking questions about me. My friends wondered what I had done. Some wrote to say they had no idea what kind of trouble I was in, but if there was any way they could help me to let them know.

The FBI was also visiting producers and implying I was guilty of something by saying, "We're investigating him and need any information you can give us."

This development was followed by mysterious threats against my life. I was called regularly in the middle of the night and told in detail how I would be killed in torturous ways. Anonymous, threatening mail arrived daily.

Under the threat of losing Lori, Rose Marie was so upset that it made our marriage even more difficult.

Feeling the need to get away from New York for a breather, Rose Marie and Lori flew down to New Orleans where I was doing the Shrine circus. The circus was good for them. They were able to forget the pressures for awhile. During our stay there, we visited the "incurable hospital," where the circus used to perform each year. As we looked around at these pitiful cases, people who would never leave that hospital, I whispered to Rose Marie, "And we think WE have troubles."

Returning to New York, new summonses awaited us.

Kidnap threats against my daughter were being added to the pressures. They came by telephone wherever I traveled. Yet I thought no one knew where I was staying when I was on the road. After a great deal of mental anguish and with some difficulty, I managed to get Lori secretly enrolled in a private Catholic school. Even though we were not Catholic, the compassionate priest, Father Johnson, agreed to take her there after I told him our story.

"We'll help you," he promised. "If someone should call, asking if she is here, we'll give them no information. Even if they come with a lawyer, they will have to first see our diocesan lawyers, and that will give you a chance to get her away safely."

I've never forgotten the good father for his vital help at that time.

Summonses were served on me almost daily, and I was in court so many times I lost count. My lawyer demanded and received a fee every time one was answered. We were constantly being hit from all directons. Soon we refused to answer our door. There was no joy in our life.

Then, one day I wound up in jail for an afternoon and was released the same day. "It was a mistake," they said unfeelingly. Bitterness, outrage, and fear became such a part of me that I started to carry a gun for protection.

The circus was no longer a refuge. Unseen eyes seemed to follow me throughout the tours. At the Holiday Inn in

Gulfport, Mississippi, my telephone again rang in the middle of the night.

"Hello, ringmaster," said the caller. "How do you expect to keep announcing the circus with your voice box cut out?"

There was a sharp click at the other end. I quickly put the receiver back on the hook, as though my threatening attacker was inside it, ready to leap into the room and carry out his threat. I hastened to the door to make sure it was double locked.

How did these people always know where I was staying? I never made any advance reservations, had taken to checking in under assumed names, and would tell no one in the circus where I stayed. I remembered that mysterious phone call from Washington, D.C., asking for Debbie on the day the President was assassinated. I had just checked in, without reservation, and had had no chance to tell anyone, including my wife, where I was. It was becoming downright alarming.

More threats that my daughter would be kidnapped and harmed were received, even though my daughter was supposedly safely tucked away in a private school. The agonizing suspense was becoming unbearable. I began having severe stomach pains.

In New York Rose Marie was going through her own hell. She finally changed the phone to an unlisted number.

Fortunately, the doors of the building in which we lived were so sturdy that it would have been next to impossible to break them down. Still, Rose was terror-stricken every time the doorbell rang and refused to answer it. She even shuddered when the phone rang, despite its being an unlisted number.

I was constantly in and out of the city, touring with the Tom Packs Circus. The general manager was Jack Leontini. Jack had been a member of naval intelligence, a wartime spy, so I felt I could talk to him about some of this. Leontini told me that the FBI had called on him in the Tom Packs office, located in the Arcade Building in St. Louis, and that the agent had asked a lot of questions about me.

Jack Leontini and I did not always agree. When Tom

Packs had died, his widow Thelma had kept the circus going and had promoted me to performance director as well as ringmaster. Jack had always had free rein, and none of his moves had ever been questioned before in the management of the circus. Now that I was performance director, and he had to share the responsibility with me, we had our artistic disagreements.

One thing I had learned, however, was that although circus people may battle each other, they will stick together against any threats from the outside world. I did respect Jack's overall intelligence, circus knowledge, and capabilities; and I trusted him.

Because I had been rushing back to New York after each tour ended, I had left my car behind and was flying to the various engagements. Following a performance in Natchez, Mississippi, Leontini came to see me. The next day, Tuesday, August 1, 1967, was a travel day, and the following day we would set up to perform in Lafayette, Louisiana.

"I want you to go to Lafayette," Leontini said.

"I don't know if I can get a plane in the morning," I replied.

"That's not necessary," he said. "You can ride with me. We'll leave around six A.M."

I could understand going in early for a TV or radio appearance, but a Shrine luncheon seemed rather useless. If the sponsors weren't sold on the show by this time, it would be too late anyway.

I was enjoying the confortable ride in his luxurious white Lincoln Continental; a tape of classical music was playing in full stereo. I glanced at my watch—eight A.M. We were on U.S. 61, one mile from St. Francisville, Louisiana. Approaching a curve, Jack slowed the car.

The sound of a gunshot split the silence of the air, and the windshield shattered in front of my face. Jack then floored the accelerator, and we sped away with squealing tires. The shot had apparently been fired from a small grove of trees near the roadside.

We arrived in Lafayette and immediately called the state police. The trooper said it was a small caliber bullet, and if it had been fired at a closer range, I might have been killed. It was the first time I actually knew my life was in danger, and I was terrified!

Back in my room that night, all the strange events began to take their toll on me. Shivering uncontrollably, I wondered, was I becoming paranoid?

Arriving back in New York, another summons awaited me, demanding another expensive court appearance. Something snapped inside of me. I had reached the breaking point. I put on my trench coat, dropped the .25-caliber automatic into my side pocket, and headed for the modeling office where I expected to find my ex-wife Debbie. I no longer cared about the consequences. It was raining. That suited my mood. I walked down the street, glassy-eyed, and boarded the subway. Everything around me seemed unreal and caricatured.

I arrived at the building and made my way upstairs. Approaching the office, I was stopped by a man at the door. I threw him up against a wall then flung open the door. The office was empty.

"I tried to tell you," said the man, quaking. "There's nobody here. They left early because of the weather. You missed them by five minutes."

I began to tremble, realizing what had almost happened. Drenched with nervous exhaustion and weak-kneed, I left the office building and walked to nearby St. Patrick's Cathedral. I fell heavily to my knees at the altar. The gun was still in my pocket.

"Lord," I prayed, "I'm desperate! I need help! Something has to give. I'm calling on You to show me a way out."

After the prayer, I settled back in the pew, thinking. There seemed to be no solution, no answer, to the problem. I was afraid if I gave up the diary I would end up dead. . . . I bolted upright in the pew as my thoughts were racing with new possibilities. Of course! That was it! That was the answer!!

# 12
# The Day I Died

"You must be crazy! You could never get away with it!" Rose Marie exclaimed incredulously as I outlined a plan to fake my death and reappear with a new identity.

"But I must," I said while pacing back and forth in our living room. "It's our last hope. First of all, I must change my name and my appearance. With my background in makeup it will be easy. I'll change my hair style and color, grow side burns, cap my teeth, and no one will recognize me. Then I will get new identification papers. I've got to make people believe I'm dead; then I'll step into my new identity."

We racked our brains for most of the night. We wanted a name that could be easily remembered. After several hours we finally agreed upon—AUSTIN MILES.

Step two was to get complete identification. I knew of no way to get a fake birth certificate, but there was one starting place. The easiest thing to get is a social security card. I made application.

My new social security card arrived as planned, and with the help of a trusted friend, my new driver's license arrived in the mail a short time later.

A musician friend from Louisiana who was aware of my problems was in complete agreement that drastic action was merited to end this deplorable situation. He offered to help. We arranged to stage a fake visit to his home with an exchange of letters. His letter to me would be an invitation to visit him over the Christmas holidays, and my reply would state my acceptance and our expected time of arrival. I was also supposed to send a telegram on the day of my departure.

On that day the plan was that I would drive my car into

a swamp along the proposed route and leave in it our luggage with clothing and papers of identification. My friend was then supposed to meet us there and wisk us away to an airport. Under different names we would fly out of the area. My friend, in the meantime, was supposed to call the state police several hours after my scheduled arrival, expressing concern and asking them to check on us. We hoped the police would eventually find the car in the swamp and assume we had died.

I left to go on a little Christmas tour. From there I planned to return to Evansville, pick up Lori, and head for our fateful visit to Louisiana.

I had just left Jacksonville, Ohio, on my way to Salem, Virginia, for a General Electric performance. I was supposed to meet some performers on the Virginia side for a bite to eat before continuing on to our destination. It was December 15, 1967.

I had just entered the area of Kanauga, Ohio, and the traffic had been thickening as I approached. By the time the bridge was in view cars were now bumper to bumper. The traffic inched slowly forward, stopped, then inched forward again. I felt my restlessness and impatience increasing. There was an unusual calm in the air, almost an eerie silence, and then, suddenly, the bridge raised up, twisting like soft taffy. Fully loaded with cars, it plunged into the river with a deafening roar. I was only three cars from the entrance to the bridge.

The people in their cars and in the shops along the road remained stunned for a few seconds. Then bedlam and panic broke loose as they came running from all directions to try to help. Feeling numb all over, I stood on the bank and watched. After having made plans to fake my death, I had barely escaped the real thing!

Deciding to take advantage of this terrible tragedy for the sake of my own life, I got into my car and drove back upstream. Taking some of my luggage from the trunk, I threw it into the river, hoping it would be found as evidence I had been on the bridge. "Kokomo, may you rest in peace," I said as the suitcases sailed through the air.

# 13
# Austin Miles Is Born

My death was indeed untimely. It wasn't supposed to occur until December 23. The death of America's leading ringmaster was picked up by the wire services, front page on some papers, and shown on several newscasts. I read my own obituary, which is a rare privilege.

I called Rose Marie and told her it was urgent for her to meet me in Indiana. When she arrived, she saw a newspaper account of my death. "My God," she said, "they put you on the front page."

Rose Marie and I discussed how she should deal with inquiries about my death and how we would blend our lives with my new identity. She returned to New York while Lori and I stayed at my mother's.

For the next three months I kept a low profile away from public view while my appearance underwent some changes. The first few days were hectic as reporters and the curious were popping into the house unexpectedly. My daughter and I hid out in the basement recreation room. The house, formerly owned by a doctor, had a bookcase that opened to a secret passageway that once had been a vault. Whenever we heard the door bell, we would race to hide behind that fake bookcase.

One day the door bell rang with more force than usual. "FBI," we heard the voice say. After the agent identified himself, my mother told him that the family was going through enough at the moment and to please come at another time.

"I can't take much more of this, son," my mother later said, the strain showing in her face. "I don't know what to say to people. Everyone has been here—Reverend Chapin, the newspapers, now the FBI. You know that Harry's not well, and he can't take the strain either."

It seemed best for my parents' sake for us to go to another location until things quieted down. We got up early one morning; I wore a disguise, a delivery man's costume with horn rimmed glasses, and Lori and I slipped away unrecognized to Kentucky. On the way Christmas carols were playing on the radio. Then there was a break in the music for the news. "So far the body of the ringmaster has not been located," said the announcer.

I felt a little weak in the stomach as I heard this account being given on the news. I felt even weaker after placing a call to my mother's home three weeks later and being told that a body had been found, and they were certain that it was mine.

There was more unfinished business to which I had to attend. I marked "deceased" on my federal income tax returns and then immediately filed my first form as Austin Miles, so there would be no lapse in my annual filing with the IRS. Every credit card bill was paid in full, then the card returned cut in half with "deceased" marked on it. These were just some of the things I had to do to give us a chance to start a new life.

It cost me dearly. I had worked for years to build a professional career. Now I had to face a new challenge by starting over. My marriage was already in shreds due, in part, to the pressure. Rose Marie and I had been married only one year and nine months.

The worst part of the situation was that I really could not explain it fully to anybody. Almost everyone in the nation trusted the FBI and those connected with the White House. I knew nobody would believe me! I really had no one to whom I could turn.

I called my mother from Kentucky, saying I was coming to see her. After I arrived home, my mother went to the store. The door bell rang. Not knowing who was on the other side, I suddenly felt uneasy. Quickly putting on my disguise, complete with horn rimmed glasses, I answered the door and met a man in his thirties wearing glasses, with dark hair, medium height, and a sturdy build.

"FBI," he said, taking out his card. I read his name, Richard Eisgruber.

When I told him I was just a visitor, he left without asking any more questions. My heart was pounding so hard I doubt if I could have answered any.

Restless, I wanted to return to work. I had built a good reputation as a ringmaster, but in show business you're only as good as your last performance, so I figured once I got started as Austin Miles, doors would open for me. Gil Gray, the circus producer, knew me, so I started with him.

"Now remember, Gil," I said in my phone call to him, "you'll have to bill me as Austin Miles."

"It makes no difference to me," Gil said. "I'll bill you as Cleopatra if you like. Just do your job; that's all that counts."

# 14

# 'By the way, Your Dad Died'

Mom had called and told me that dad's health was declining, so I decided to go to Indiana during a two week break in the circus. I phoned to let her know what time my plane would get in.

Within an hour after I arrived home, Lori and I were unpacking our clothes when we heard voices outside. We glanced out the upstairs window. My dad was working quietly on his car and had suddenly been intruded upon. I recognized the man talking to him; it was Richard Eisgruber from the FBI.

My dad, a most gentle soul, was very upset and began to raise his voice. "Look, I've said everything to you that I'm going to say. Now I'm telling you to leave me alone!"

Anger stirred within me. Here was my dad, who was ill, being harassed because of his association with me.

Later I said to my mom, "I tell you, our telephone is bugged. Everytime I call you to tell you I'm coming home, Eisgruber shows up."

"Son," she said with concern, "you're imagining things. This is America. Why, things like that don't happen here."

I gave up, unable to think of any way to make her understand.

My circus tours were now taking me across the United States and back. About the only area of each city I got to know was the stretch between the hotel and the arena, with side jaunts to the local radio and TV stations.

Before long my dad's health was deteriorating again, and I took advantage of the next break in my schedule to go home. I called my mother from the road to tell her I was on my way and my arrival time. Within the hour the door bell rang. I was upstairs. It was Richard Eisgruber.

My mother had now reached the breaking point. "Yes, he's here," she said. She called upstairs for me to come down.

"He's really here?" Eisgruber asked, almost in disbelief.

"Are you ––?" he demanded, calling me by my real name.

"Hold it," I countered before answering. "Show me your credentials."

Eisgruber showed us his identification.

"Yes, I am he," I replied, thereby blowing my cover and identity change.

"I'd like to ask you some questions," he said.

"I don't want to answer questions," I replied hotly.

My mother was disturbed. At this point she admonished me.

I tried once again to feebly explain. But how could she ever understand? She loved her country and was very naive when it came to politics.

"Something else I want to know," she said, turning to the agent. "The FBI hasn't bugged our telephone, have they?" She was so apple pie innocent.

"Why of course not, madam. Why would we do a thing like that?"

"There, you see, son. I don't know what has happened to you."

I threw my hands up in despair. What could I do?

Eisgruber then began to ask pointless questions. "Where have you been working? What have you been doing?"

"It's none of your d– business," I told him flatly.

Finally I said, "Look, Eisgruber, why don't you get to the point? What is it you really want?"

"There are a few things about your divorce we need to know."

"I knew it! Mom, this proves it. There is no way the FBI gets involved with a divorce case." I was furious.

"Please," my mother interrupted. "My son has been under a terrible strain. Please accept our apologies; he is not himself. Maybe it would be better if we didn't talk any more. I'm sorry. There's always been peace in this house."

As Eisgruber left, I held the door, glaring at him.

Back in New York Rose Marie found new difficulty in our life together because of our double identity. She was known by one name to our neighbors and by another in public. It was obvious that my marriage had deteriorated. And her resentment of me continued to grow. Rose Marie would not travel with me or even visit me for a weekend on the road and was more and more often not at home when I returned.

One of the low points of our relationship came when I returned from a tour to an empty apartment. Rose Marie was out. An opened telegram was on the desk on top of a pile of mail. I read it, and I felt my insides break apart. My dad had died. As I sat staring at it, the telephone rang. It was Rose Marie. She carried on a conversation for a few minutes about when she would be home. Then she said, casually, "Oh, by the way, your dad died."

"By the way," I said in disbelief. "Is that all you have to say?"

My daughter came home from school. "Honey," I said, trying to hold back tears, "we have to talk. This is a big chair discussion." From the time she was tiny, we had a big leather chair, and anytime there was need for a "father and daughter" talk, or a really serious discussion, that would be a "big chair discussion."

When I told her that grandaddy had been called home to heaven, she managed to hold back her tears. We just both sat there silently. I made arrangements to fly out later that night to Evansville. I had missed the funeral, but I did want to go as quickly as possible to be with my mother during her time of grief.

When I arrived in Evansville, I was surprised at how my mother had changed. Her face was tired and drawn looking. She had found dad after his attack lying in a pool of blood on the bathroom floor. He had been fine when she left him earlier in the day.

I had to fly to Wichita, Kansas, for a performance that night. The Masonic cemetery is at the end of the airport runway, and as the plane lifted into the air, I could see dad's grave with the fresh flowers on top.

# 15

# Jack Anderson Threatens FBI

In the midst of the gaiety of the circus, still grieving over the death of my dad, I learned a letter writing campaign had begun. Anti-American notes, signed with my name, had been mailed to prominent columnists—Jack O'Brien, Earl Wilson, and others.

In New York City I ran into Johnny Woods, an announcer, who seemed overjoyed to tell me that he had been at the recent Shriners convention, that the FBI had been there asking questions about me, and that the Shriners were having second thoughts about having me with their circuses. I knew then that this matter could go on no longer.

I called the Federal Bureau of Investigation headquarters in Washington, D.C., person-to-person to J. Edgar Hoover. The receptionist said it would not be possible to talk to him but that she would put the call through to Thomas B. Coll, Hoover's right-hand man. I told him who I was and that I had been under harassment from the FBI.

"I'm coming to Washington tomorrow on the eleven o'clock Eastern shuttle from New York," I said, "and from there, I'm coming directly to headquarters. And I'm telling you, SOMEBODY is going to talk to me and explain a few things, and I mean it!"

"I'll talk to you myself when you get here," Coll said.

Next, I called Jack Anderson, the "Washington Merry-Go-Round" national columnist, and told him about the diary, what it contained, how the FBI had been hounding me, and about the attempt upon my life. We made arrangements to meet before I was to go to the FBI headquarters.

Then I called Earl Wilson, a columnist friend of mine.

"I'm glad you called," Earl said. "Frankly, I had gotten pretty sore at you after I got that letter."

I nearly exploded with rage when he informed me of its contents. "Earl, I did *not* write that letter!"

Similar letters were also sent to other columnists.

"I'm taking the diary to Jack Anderson, and I am meeting with Thomas Coll at FBI headquarters. This diary could blow Washington wide open."

Earl told me to use his direct line phone number and said to call him as soon as I returned from Washington. I felt by the tone of his voice that he thought the entire story was incredible.

The next morning I was on the nine o'clock shuttle for Washington. As the plane carried me and the diary toward the nation's capital, many unanswered questions floated through my thoughts. Who was behind the constant harassment I had faced? Who had supplied Debbie with the money for a change of venue from New York to Las Vegas and then for her to go to Las Vegas from New York and set up her required residency and have an attorney end our marriage so quietly? Who had called my mother and told her in a threatening way to tell me to forget the entire matter? Why had I been shot at once, but never again?

As the plane made its approach to Washington International Airport, I couldn't help but wonder if the FBI had overzealously stepped beyond the power normally entrusted to them, or was it simply the wish of J. Edgar Hoover to obtain that diary with all its sexual perversion to give him extra power over the White House?

Who would have the power, money, and influence to follow every move I had made? Who had tried to shoot me? Why? If I had died, what would that have gained them without the diary?

I shuddered when I thought of all the prominent names listed in the diary. The culprit behind the scenes could have been any one of them.

I anxiously wondered how Jack Anderson would handle the situation.

It was indeed a sad state of affairs. The time bomb I was

carrying could go off any day, and my entire family could be blown to bits with the repercussions from the explosion. As the old saying goes, I was damned if I did and damned if I didn't. But, I had finally been pushed to the point where I had to *do* something.

Today I would face Jack Anderson and then the FBI. I looked thoughtfully out the window of the plane. The sky was blue and endless. Enormous white clouds seemed to engulf the airship at intervals, entrapping my thoughts like a dream. Looking out on the vastness of the sky, I suddenly felt very minute. "God," I whispered to myself, "please guide my footsteps. Help me to make the right decisions and get this life of mine straightened out. I don't know where else to turn." My eyes closed in fervent prayer, hoping for some sort of divine intervention. A calmness descended upon me and with it a quiet determination.

When I met Jack Anderson and Britt Hume in their office, I was relieved to hand over the diary. Carrying the dangerous documentation in my attache case had made me nervous. Even as they thumbed through the first pages, their eyes widened in amazement.

It was now time for me to go to FBI headquarters. As I went into the lobby, I was asked to open my attaché case. Then I was passed through to the elevator and upstairs to the office of Thomas B. Coll.

He was all polish—an extremely tall man and well groomed. "How do you do, Mr. Miles," he said pleasantly. "Right after your call, I made a check of our files and even a cross-check in the central files and have found absolutely nothing. Why, you're not under investigation by the FBI, Mr. Miles. We have absolutely nothing on you to warrant an investigation."

"Well, sir, a lot of people sure seem to think I am, at Shrine conventions, producers' offices, and every other place where I have business dealings!"

"Mr. Miles," he repeated sternly, "you are not under FBI investigation. Somebody is kidding you."

"Since so many people think that I am under investigation, and it is hurting my career, will you be good enough to give me a statement on FBI stationery stating I am not under investigation?"

He flatly refused.

"How about your Evansville, Indiana, agent named Richard Eisgruber?" I asked.

"Eisgruber? Richard Eisgruber?" He looked at the papers on his desk. "We have no agent by the name of Richard Eisgruber that I know of."

"Mr. Coll, I saw his credentials," I replied indignantly.

He frowned as he said, "You know it is highly possible that the credentials were fake!"

"Mr. Coll, this man showed up at my home every time I called. He knew exactly when I was arriving at my mother's home every time I visited her. Finally, when I did talk to him, he took down notes. Now, why would an imposter do that?"

He shook his head as if to say he didn't know.

"And one of your agents in St. Louis did not contact my boss, Jack Leontini?"

"Mr. Miles, I don't know what kind of joke people are playing on you, but I've told you before, we are not investigating you; and furthermore, you never have been investigated by the FBI."

"You're a d– liar, Mr. Coll!"

The G-man was taken aback, indignation on his face.

"I once applied for USO papers and was investigated by the FBI. They told me I would have to have FBI clearance before I could go."

Coll started to rise from his seat, an entirely new expression on his face.

As he started to rise, I started to rise with him. "By the way, Mr. Coll. Just before coming to this office, I was with Jack Anderson. He knows I am here. I left the diary with him. So if I'm not back in his office within the hour, he'll know right where to look, and you can bet that diary will be all over the world in tomorrow's papers."

Thomas B. Coll remained suspended half way between a sitting and a standing position, still holding the arms of his chair. His reaction confirmed my suspicion that he knew about the diary and my connection with it. I remained in the exact same position, staring directy at him. With great, trained control Thomas Coll slowly reseated himself. With relief I said, "Good day, Mr. Coll," as I made my way to the door. I was impressed by the power of Anderson's name to intimidate public figures and was grateful for it at this moment.

When I arrived back in Jack Anderson's office, I related the exact conversation which had occurred at the FBI office. I found they had managed to go through quite a bit of the diary. As they came to one page, Britt Hume exclaimed incredulously, "I can't believe it. All this stuff happening right down the street at the White House!"

Then I gave Mr. Hume the name and number of a dancer who had participated in the sex orgies at the White House and who had agreed to be a witness.

I was with Britt Hume and Jack Anderson for six hours. At the end of the day Jack Anderson said to Britt Hume, "I'm going to make a call over to FBI headquarters and let them know I have the diary, and if they make any more trouble for Miles, we'll publish it." Anderson went to his desk and made the call.

As soon as I returned to New York, I called Earl Wilson. Later he did further research on his own. In his book, *Show Business Laid Bare,* Putnam Publishers, Earl gives even more details of the "sex-capades" and shenanigans at the White House, many of which coincided with events outlined in the diary.

# 16
# Pillow of Stone

As the mule I was riding wound its way upward around the mountain near the Diros Caves in Greece, it seemed oblivious to the narrow path rimming the mountain, which was banked on one side by the steep rise of the hill and on the other with a sheer drop of several hundred feet to jagged rock formations below. Straining at each rise in the pathway, the little mule walked dangerously close to the edge. Several rocks slipped over the side. I looked down at my foot. It was suspended in space!

"Why does this confounded animal have to walk on the very edge of this path?" I thought. Although I had never heard of a mule and rider plunging over one of these cliffs, I did not want to be the first.

As we slowly gained altitude, the panoramic view of the hills dazzled my senses. Between two mountains, a valley seemed to stretch into infinity, yet I knew we were not too far from the sea.

I halted the mule for a few moments, intrigued by the silence. There was life all around, yet the atmosphere was hushed. Never before had I experienced such solitude. Acclimated as I was to the cacophony of continuous sounds in New York, the extreme quiet was actually an assault on my ears, reminding me of the quotation, the silence was deafening. It was just such quiet solitude that I had traveled so far to seek. I gave the mule a gentle nudge with my heels, and we proceeded. Taking a deep breath of the fresh air, I began to reflect on the extraordinary events that had brought me to this place.

Although my professional career as Austin Miles was

advancing steadily, I had a gnawing feeling inside that God wanted me to serve Him. It had begun to dominate my thoughts to such an extent that I felt a decision needed to be made.

As I approached my destination, the form of a building hewed out of stone seemed to grow right out of the mountain top. Indeed, this was the very idea of the original monks who had retreated here. Many of the rooms inside were natural stone caves.

After being greeted by the abbott, I was shown to the cell which would be my home for the next several days. A stone would be my pillow. It was to be a time of total silence, meditation, and prayer.

Men of all ages and backgrounds were in the monastery. I had the feeling that some were trying to buy back their souls. Perhaps this was one reason we were not permitted to speak. Each man's privacy was secured so that nothing would distract him as he was seeking God. Conversation would have been difficult anyway, for it seemed no two people were from the same country. Language would have been a barrier.

There was a comfort being there with one another, knowing that basically we were all seeking the same thing—God's will in our lives.

Adjusting to this monastic way of life was most difficult. My mind ran in all directions, but by the third day I was developing the attitude of a contemplative and was able to keep my mind and thoughts focused on Jesus. It was then that He spoke to my heart. "Son, when you give yourself fully to me, I put my arms around you like a protective umbrella. As long as you do those things which are pleasing in my sight, every promise in the Bible is yours."

I had come to the right place to search my mind and examine my heart! In that little chapel in the monastery on the mountain, I reset the priorities in my life and vowed, "Yes, Jesus, I will serve you. I will take any path you choose for me."

# 17
# The Key . . . to the Kingdom

". . . Therefore, Mr. Miles, the city of New Orleans is proud to present you with this certificate of honorary citizenship and the key to the city."

The audience of 7,500 applauded as the mayor's representative made the presentation in the center ring of the Municipal Auditorium. There was no hiding the happiness in my face. I was the *first* ringmaster to ever receive such an award. Every facet of my career was zooming upward, receiving national recognition. I was proud of my accomplishment, and I loved the circus. God had answered my prayers, and now I had an obligation to fulfill.

I sought out Ike Chapman, the publicity agent for the circus. "Ike," I said, "is there a religious radio station in town?"

"I'm not sure, but I'll check," he said.

"Please do. This will be a personal favor, apart from the circus. I'll appreciate whatever you can do."

Ike found a Christian station in the area and arranged for me to be interviewed on the air by Mr. Ford, the program director.

After an elaborate introduction Mr. Ford asked me to tell the radio audience something about the circus.

To his surprise I said, "I didn't come here to plug the circus; I came to talk about God."

I gave my testimony sincerely, giving God credit for the transformation in my life.

In a nearby announcer's booth a man listening to tapes glanced up. Through the plate glass window he could see my interview being conducted in the main studio. He flipped off his tape and glanced over at the staff announcer. "Is it possible to pipe that interview in here? I'd like to hear what's going on."

"Sure," said the announcer as he flipped a switch.

The man put his elbow on the console, resting his chin in his hand, listening intently and studying me through the glass.

The program director finished the interview, saying, "I never thought I would live to see the day when a circus ringmaster would refuse to talk about the circus and dwell instead on Jesus." He smiled teasingly, "We're surely in the last days."

No sooner had he thanked me than approving listeners began to telephone the studio.

As we were leaving the main room, the man in the announcer's booth hurriedly got to his feet and came directly to me, extending his hand.

"Praise the Lord," he said exuberantly. "I just listened to your interview. My name's Coleman McDuff. I'm an evangelist, and I'm having a crusade at the Westwego Assembly of God Church. Would it be possible for you to come Sunday morning and give your testimony? I think it would sure bless a lot of people."

There was no way I could know that this chance encounter would provide me with the greatest challenges and victories yet to come—and that my future life would hinge on that sensitive evangelist who followed a "leading" of the Lord.

"Yes," I found myself answering, "I would be happy to come. What time's the service?" I was thinking about my scheduled matinee at 1:45.

Service starts at eleven," the evangelist said, shaking my hand. "It usually gets over around 12:30, but it's so far to the circus at Municipal Auditorium, you probably won't have a chance to get lunch before the show."

"I'll skip a meal for God anytime," I said.

Coleman shook my hand again, his mouth turning up in a warm grin.

On Sunday morning a young man picked me up at my

hotel for the trip to the Westwego church. As I entered, loud sounds of fervent prayer filled the air. The pastor's voice predominated. People were praying openly, some with audible words and some with strange sounds, while many had their hands lifted high in the air. It seemed a far departure from my former staid Presbyterian and Methodist background. Yet, after the events that had happened in that circus tent when the dying man was "prayed" back to life and the Divine protection I felt God had given me after my change of identity, I was completely open to any work of God. I didn't fully understand everything that was taking place, but then, can anybody understand God and His works in their totality?

The prayer ended with a congregational hymn. Coleman spotted me in the back and, motioning me to the platform, gestured for me to be seated next to the pastor, Paul Radke, a husky man whose head was bowed in prayer. As I quietly sat down next to him, he opened his eyes. Keeping his head in a bowed position, he tilted it slightly toward me. A smile flashed on his face as he squeezed my arm in welcome.

Sensing my nervousness, Coleman McDuff sat next to me and said, "Now don't worry about what you're going to say. Just let the Holy Spirit guide your words, and keep your mind on Christ."

I gave my first testimony that morning, using a Bible my mother had given me for Christmas when I was twelve years old. There was a glow and inner peace I had never felt before.

Pastor Radke asked if I would come back the following Sunday morning. My affirmative response was immediate.

"What are your plans?" Reverend Radke asked me the next Sunday.

"I feel God has called me to the ministry," I said spontaneously.

"Well," the Reverend said matter of factly, "I have some books I want to give you to begin your studies. When do you leave to go back to New York?"

"My plane leaves tonight after the last show," I replied. "I have a show in New York tomorrow night."

"I can't get them for you until tomorrow," he said. "Is there any way you can stay over?"

Checking the airport for the next day's flights, I found every plane booked solid; yet, I felt so strongly that God wanted me to have those books that, taking a chance, I picked out a morning flight and asked to be put on stand-by. The next morning Reverend Radke drove me to the airport. He had given me several study books and information concerning the Berean Bible School, where I could earn my degree by correspondence. Before I left the car at the airport, Reverend Radke held my hand and gave special prayer for me. I had no doubt the Lord had arranged my meeting with Reverend Radke.

During the final boarding, at the very last minute, one seat became available on the plane, and I arrived in New York on time for the show.

# 18
# Healed

Studying for the ministry occupied every moment of my spare time. Not only did I discover a deep joy in the Bible as a "now" book, but I was finding extra pleasure in my circus work as well. The press was being particularly kind to me, and the country had accepted Austin Miles, the ringmaster.

I was now appearing on major TV shows, such as "Mike Douglas" and "To Tell The Truth." Walter Cronkite and Harry Reasoner filmed me for their national newscasts introducing Karl Wallenda on one of his many "farewell" appearances. I appeared in educational films, guest shots in movies, and TV roles. Between tours there were circus lectures at women's clubs, in museums, and before civic groups. Joe Franklin continued to invite me as a guest on his New York TV celebrity show whenever I was in town.

Since the Tom Packs Circus played to audiences of 10,000 to 35,000 at each performance, a diversity of well-known people became available for guest spots to be introduced by me to these huge crowds. I was, however, thoroughly unprepared to greet one particular guest who had made himself available for this honor.

On this day, Senator Quinn, chairman of the Spencer, Massachusetts, fair where we were to perform, had met me for breakfast in his hotel to plan out our day.

"Ted Kennedy's coming by today," the Senator said. "He'll come to the stage so you can introduce him at the beginning of the show."

I almost choked on my coffee.

When Senator Quinn left, I was glad to be alone for a few moments to recover. Ted Kennedy, of all people! How ironic! The name brought to mind all the old hurts. It had been some time since John and Bobby Kennedy had been assassinated and the New York modeling agency had suddenly vanished, leaving no trace of the models or other personnel.

Now I was to come face to face with one of those who had caused those painful years. I couldn't help but be apprehensive as I waited.

The entire area around the stage had been roped off and was heavily guarded. The stage itself was separated from the grandstand by a race track. Sirens wailed in the distance. As the police escort stopped outside the ropes, there was a roar from the crowd. Kennedy ducked under the ropes along with the two secret service men. Strangely, they kept their distance from him. He was walking alone across the grassy area toward me when our eyes met. As he approached the stage area, I moved a few steps toward him. We both stopped, face to face. Then, like robots programmed for polite reaction, our hands automatically reached for each other's. After a brief speech, he very formally turned the mike back to me, and the circus began.

In Birmingham, Alabama, when I introduced George Wallace, a member of the Shrine Temple, there was sheer bedlam for twenty minutes as the crowd cheered, threw hats in the air, and gave rebel yells.

Carl Stokes, the nation's first black mayor, was my guest in Cleveland. I made him an honorary ringmaster. He was given a rousing, thunderous reception that would rival that of any film or TV star. When I gave him the whistle, which he blew to start the show, he trotted across the ring to his convertible and with unseen wings leaped in the air, cleared the top, and landed in the back seat.

During intermission Stokes, an animal lover, asked to see the circus menagerie. Along with his two body guards we went to find the animals. He was fascinated with the elephants and moved right in next to them to pat their trunks. The body guards, who had kept their distance, became more and more exasperated. Finally, one blurted out loudly, "Don't expect us to protect you from THEM!"

My next accomplishment was the creation of a "Ringmaster's Award," a silver chain and whistle, for individuals in public life who exemplified high standards of conduct. Each candidate was carefully chosen for giving of himself to help others. Charlton Heston was the first to be so honored. Singer Ricky Nelson also became a recipient.

Among others so honored were a heroic fire chief in Maine who saved a child from a burning house and retiring Governor Dempsey of Connecticut for his unpublicized work with the retarded.

The presentation of this award brought such favorable publicity to the recipients that it soon became much sought after. I had finally made it to the very top of my profession.

It was during our Southern tour that I became increasingly aware of many nagging aches and pains and noticed a rapid weight loss. After one grueling performance, my midsection wracked with pain, I hurried to my dressing room where I slumped to the floor. To my horror I noticed a pool of blood forming beneath me. At the hospital a new shock awaited me—the dreaded diagnosis, cancer! It was so far advanced that I was flown home to New York City where my doctor made arrangements for my admission to Sloan Kettering Memorial Hospital.

Waiting at home, I looked in the mirror. My cheeks were sunken and hollow, and the face that stared back at me expressed the gloom that only someone with a terminal illness could appreciate.

Suddenly it occurred to me. I had tried God before. Why not now? Excited with the hope of this new possibility, I asked my daughter's piano teacher if she knew if there was an evangelist with gifts of healing in New York City. Sure enough, a service was being held in a downtown hotel.

At the meeting the minister prayed for me. Home that evening after hours of excruciating pain, I finally fell asleep. Sometime in the middle of the night, the bed began to shake, and I was awakened three different times with a deep warmth flowing through my body. In the morning as the sunlight bathed the room, the realization that my body was no longer in pain flooded my consciousness. I literally bounced out of bed. The same mirror that had gloomily reflected my ashen face the day before now beamed back a rosy bright-eyed countenance.

Happily, I called for my daughter. As Lori entered the bedroom, her eyes widened in astonishment. "Praise the Lord, daddy!"

"Yes, praise the Lord, Lori—I'm healed!"

We both cried and laughed as we danced merrily around the room. Rose Marie just shook her head in disbelief.

A subsequent visit to the doctor and new tests confirmed the fact that the cancer was gone. Overwhelmed by gratitude for God's answer to yet another prayer, I vowed again that my life would be dedicated to serving Him wherever and whenever I could.

Austin and Shriners on a movie set with Charlton Heston who is wearing the "Ringmaster's Award" around his neck.

# 19

# God's Uneasy Instrument

The outrageous thought of presenting a circus on a concert hall stage crossed my mind. Why not?

The idea intrigued me. Using acts and talent equipped to play a proscenium stage, I would create a "circus fantasy."

While putting this together, I encountered Leonard Green, Emmett Kelly, Jr.'s, manager, who had been looking for a good vehicle for Emmett. He had contacts I needed, and my ideas and contacts were valuable to him. Furthermore, he was willing to invest some of his own money, as I would be doing. The Emmett Kelly, Jr., Circus evolved. I went to work immediately, creating special numbers for Emmett. One was a ballet with Emmett and Raggedy Ann. Gentle Ben, the bear of television fame, was chosen as the star animal attraction. Everything came together for a beautiful performance.

One week before we were to open our road tour, the office was a scurry of activity as thousands of last minute arrangements were being made. Six conversations were going on at once when the telephone rang.

"Hi, Brother Austin," said the friendly voice with the unmistakable Texas accent. "This is Coleman McDuff."

Coleman was holding an evangelistic crusade at Calvary Temple Assembly of God Church in Springfield, Missouri.

"You've been on my heart for several weeks," Coleman continued. "I really feel you would be a blessing out here. There are a lot of young people attending the crusade who need direction. Could you possibly fly out and give your testimony tomorrow night? The church will pay your plane fare and expenses, and give you an honorarium."

I was so naive in religious terminology that I thought an

"honorarium" was a mention in the newspaper.

It was interesting that Coleman should have had me on his heart so long. What he did not know was that since I had first met him, I had been miraculously healed of cancer.

To the consternation of the entire production staff, I flew out the next day to spend that night in church.

In Springfield I discovered that my coming had been well publicized in the local papers; even the local TV newscasts gave it mention. Apparently a converted circus ringmaster was quite a curiosity. The publicity brought out a number of "circus aficionados." As I looked out over the congregation, I saw circus people I had known personally. They had always known me as a quiet loner; now they were here to see another side of me.

After the preliminaries of the service, Pastor Stewart Robinson rose to introduce me. Pastor Robinson, a good-looking man, richly dressed, with light hair, told something of my background. In an attempt to look after my interest, he said, "This man has come all the way from New York. Now it costs money for his plane fare and expenses, and his time is valuable. So we want to be sure to be really generous. Those of you who wish may write checks."

My heart sank. Several of the people I knew from the circus nodded their heads as if to say, "Miles has a pretty good thing going with religion." To them it was all a con game, anyway.

I winced inwardly. Nevertheless, the people responded as the pastor had asked. They gave generously, without even hearing me speak. My ministry hadn't yet been proven.

"If one soul should be turned off tonight because of this," I thought, "then I have wasted God's time and mine. It would have been far better had I not come at all. Please, Lord, this may be the only chance I will ever have to reach this particular gathering" was my quiet prayer. I knew there might be someone there who had never gone to church but had been attracted by the publicity to come tonight. I could not afford the chance of having anyone turn away from God because of the appeal which had been made for me. Every life, every soul, was vital.

I took the pulpit and thanked the congregation for their generous response to support me. "You'll never know how much I appreciate the fact you are willing to give support to me. However, I am working in the circus where the Lord is providing for me. I'm so grateful for His care that I'm going to turn this offering back to the church."

Pastor Robinson's mouth dropped open in surprise. People in the congregation seemed to sit up with a new expectancy, especially the circus people. I felt their hearts were now open to hear the Gospel. The barriers were down.

I told the congregation how God had initially made me aware of His presence by healing a heart attack victim during a circus performance. "And something you don't know about, Coleman," I said, looking over at him. "Three months ago, God divinely healed me of cancer!"

Coleman's eyes widened as he remembered that I had been very much on his mind and in his prayers. He hadn't known why.

Great excitement built in the congregation as I went on to tell them of my healing. I had struck a responsive chord.

When I finished speaking, Pastor Robinson rose and said, "There is a man here who has the same problem you had, Austin. God surely had His hand in this! His name is A. J. Clark, vice president of one of our banks. He isn't a member of this church, but he is very much loved in this community, and we would like you to pray for him."

Before I could say anything, one of the ushers brought Mr. Clark forward for prayer. As they were coming down the aisle, I prayed, "Dear God, *I* have no gift of healing. What do I do now?" I had only come to speak. I knew nothing about praying for the sick.

While Mr. Clark and the usher were making their way to the platform, a biblical statement by the Apostle Paul flashed through my mind. "God is faithful, who will not suffer you to be tempted above that ye are able . . ." (1 Cor. 10:13). I quickly reasoned that if God won't suffer us to be tempted beyond what we can bear, then He won't put us in a situation we can't handle *when* we are in His will. Certainly I was in His will by being here.

By now the man was standing before me. I reached out and placed my hands on him, praying for his healing. "Guide my prayer," I silently begged the Holy Spirit.

"Praise God in advance," I said, "and accept your healing because it has already been provided for on Calvary. Hold on to your healing. Don't let anyone talk you out of it. You'll find many logical minds that will try to convince you that God doesn't heal."

I remembered how Rose Marie had reacted when I returned from the prayer meeting where my own healing was initiated. She had challenged me with every doubt she could conceive.

"It is written in Scripture," I continued confidently, "that 'I am the Lord that healeth thee . . . I will take sickness away from the midst of thee . . . the prayer of faith shall save the sick, and the Lord shall raise him up.' In the name of Jesus, I take authority over the disease in this body and command it to be healed!"

Many people's hearts were touched by the service, and the altar was filled with people kneeling and weeping. Many dedicated themselves to Jesus. One, a school teacher with tears in his eyes, said to me, "I must admit, I was skeptical about you at first, but that really did it for me when you turned back the collection to the church." The teacher accepted Jesus into his life. That soul may have been lost had I not taken the action I did.

Later, in the pastor's study, Reverend Steward Robinson said, "Look, I know you meant well out there about the money, but let me give you this." He had just finished writing and pushed toward me a check for two hundred dollars.

"Thank you, pastor," I said reaching for a pen, "but what I did out there I meant. I'm endorsing this check back to you."

On the way back to my motel after the service, I became increasingly uneasy about the unplanned healing service. There had been no physical evidence at the service that anything had taken place in the man's body. I had turned to the pastor and Coleman and said, "Could we have a word of prayer together? I want to continue to uphold Mr. Clark in prayer."

"It's quite a burden for you, isn't it?" Coleman McDuff asked with understanding.

"Yes, it is," I answered. "That man is depending upon my faith and my relationship with God to help bring about his healing. It's a tremendous responsibility."

I felt very uneasy and inadequate being placed in the role of God's healing agent. We prayed together for Mr. Clark, and I flew back to New York.

Our tour with the Emmett Kelly, Jr., Circus began a few weeks later. I received a report that Mr. Clark was improving; the doctor had discontinued his medication. Six weeks later I received word that he was completely healed. His doctor had said, "Mr. Clark had the worst case of prostate cancer I have seen in a fifty-year-old man in my twenty-five years of practice. I must tell you, I'm astonished!"

Let me confess that I too was astonished. It was then I realized that while God is ready to answer our prayers for healing, He acts on His timetable and not ours. Later I would learn that some healings come instantly; others come over a period of time. The fact that I had been permitted to act as one of His instruments of healing was to me the most mind bending and staggering part of the whole episode.

# 20

# I Couldn't Say "No"

The Emmett Kelly, Jr., Circus did not do as well financially as we had expected, but with its uniqueness and excellent critical reviews, we received national attention that would help in the future. First we were spotlighted on the ABC-TV news; then came an invitation to perform in the East Room of the White House. Erasing earlier memories of a different regime in the Executive Mansion, the new offer delighted me.

"No, I won't go with you," Rose Marie said flatly when I shared the news with her. "I can't stand Nixon. I could not bow and be nice to him!"

"Rose," I pleaded, wanting her to share in this honor, "instead of being so judging, you should welcome the opportunity of meeting a man who will be a part of history. Please consider that it's the office that's inviting us, the highest office in America."

She still refused to go.

The performance in the East Room went well, gaining our circus national publicity on television and in newspapers. I had been given VIP treatment, brought to and from the airport in a chauffeured White House limousine. It seemed a shame not to have someone sharing this occasion with me. Then we were invited back for another performance on the lawn for the annual Easter egg roll.

"Do bring your wife and daughter," Tricia Nixon Cox urged.

Rose Marie was more adamant than ever in her refusal to come. This was an experience I especially wanted my daughter to have. On tour right up to Easter, I zipped back into New York to get Lori, only to find no one home. Rose had taken Lori with her, without telling me, to the Island of Martinique in the West Indies for her Easter vacation. Once again I was alone on a holiday.

The Emmett Kelly, Jr., Circus improved its status when its fame reached the ears of Kodak, which decided to use us on a major national TV commercial selling the Kodak XL movie camera. I was the ringmaster extolling the virtues of the camera, as Emmett demonstrated the use of the camera by taking movies of our circus. Titled "Springtime in the Circus," it was scheduled to play nationally for the month of April but went so well that it was extended month by month through September. We were paid residuals every time it played.

At the International Headquarters of the Assemblies of God located in Springfield, Missouri, several key members of the head office who had attended my service at Calvary Temple quickly spread the word around the third floor executive offices about my conversion and healing of cancer. I was not then a member of the Assemblies of God, nor was I seeking to be ordained with them. I had received ministerial credentials from an independent church in Dallas, Texas, in 1969. The ordination card I had been supplied was sufficient to get me into hospitals at any hour and into prisons where I would be able to expand my Christian witnessing.

One of the ways in which the Assemblies of God raised funds was through the offer of "witnessing booklets" which contained stories of celebrities who professed to be "born-again." These attention-getting tiny booklets were sent to those who sent in a donation to "Revivaltime," the Assemblies of God radio program which was broadcast over 650 stations.

My story was a double-barreled one which combined a "born-again" experience with a Divine healing. Reverend Lee Shultz, director of communications, asked Coleman McDuff and Pastor Stewart Robinson to arrange a meeting with me. They persuaded me that my story would help many people gain faith.

I agreed to return to Springfield for the interview when

I had a two week break in the midst of a demanding, hectic schedule. They flew me in from New York, and I was given the red carpet treatment. The first person I was taken to meet was the Reverend Thomas Zimmerman, the spiritual leader of the Assemblies of God Fellowship and the World Pentecostal Fellowship. I was ushered into his ultra-plush office. He was impeccably dressed, his striking white hair perfectly barbered. He rose quickly from his desk, made his way gracefully around it, took my hand, and gave me a warm "pentecostal hug." He radiated a smooth, spellbinding charm. I found myself in awe of this man of God. Suddenly I felt very humbled.

"What a great pleasure it is to meet you, Brother Miles. I've heard so much about you," Reverend Zimmerman said with a smile. "They tell me we are going to feature your story in our new miniature booklet. I just know it's going to be a real blessing. Now if there is ever anything I can personally do for you, don't hesitate to call me."

My taped interview with C. M. Ward and Lee Shultz would be edited down and printed into a booklet they decided to name, "The Ringmaster Meets Jesus."

Taped sermons by C. M. Ward and record albums were given to me as gifts, along with a handful of other miniature booklets. Pastor Stewart Robinson invited me to his home for dinner and later drove me to the airport.

"I have a burden in my heart," he revealed to me after dinner. "I'm getting ready to make a move. I was over in Africa visiting a missionary, and while there I saw thousands of people come from the most remote areas to hear the word of Jesus. One pregnant woman carried a child and walked seven miles each way to hear a service. That woman, with tears in her eyes, said, 'Please, tell me more about your Jesus.' The people are so hungry that I feel a call to go there." He had obviously been deeply touched by his experience.

I looked around the richly furnished house the church had given him. He drove an expensive car and had the finest clothing. He obviously had a wealthy church and made a good salary. "What about all this?" I asked.

"It means nothing to me," he said with sincerity. "God

just loaned it to me for the time I was here. I must go where I feel the Lord wants me."

I was very moved. He would give up his comfortable lifestyle to go live in a simple hut in a foreign country just to preach the Gospel? I'd met some of the biggest names in the world. "But now," I reasoned, "for the first time, I'm meeting truly great men."

During the flight back to New York I dug out some of the miniature booklets from my attaché case. I jumped straight out of my seat when I found the booklet with the "Christian testimony" of J. Edgar Hoover.

I wondered how the Assemblies of God could publish a "Christian testimony" of a man who, in my opinion, seemed to be the very antithesis of what Christian standards advocate. The booklet bothered me, because, after all, they were making one about me, too!

I had occasion to visit headquarters several times while my miniature booklet was being put together. Each time I was in the vicinity Reverend Thomas Zimmerman made a special point to greet me. He appeared to me to be the most loving, charming, godly man on earth.

About this time I began to have the strong urge to enter a theological seminary. Rose Marie reacted with rage when I told her my plans to become a minister.

"If you quit the circus, then you do it without a wife!"

"Rose Marie, the set up is perfect," I replied, trying to reassure her. "The seminary is for men like myself who feel the calling to the ministry later in life. Most are my age and married, so they have living facilities for families. We could be together!"

"And how do you intend to pay for all this?" she asked.

"Every radio station in the area has offered a part-time job. I will still be earning a good salary."

"You seem to forget that I have my job here. I cannot leave New York," she said, determinedly.

"Hang that job!" I said, rising from my chair. "That's been one of the biggest barriers between us. You never want to go anywhere with me. You don't need to work. For the first time we can all be together as a family!"

"Well, I'm not giving it up. I've worked too long to give up my retirement benefits."

"Rose Marie," I pursued, in a discussion that clearly was leading nowhere, "I can be a good husband to you and make you happy if you will only give me a chance. We don't even know each other. Even if you don't . . . love me, you must recognize that God has worked miracles for us."

"There you go with that Jesus business again," she retorted bitterly.

"Rose, I know I could be an excellent minister."

"You could be good in whatever you made up your mind to do," she said in a surprising mixed compliment, "but I did not marry a minister; I would never marry a minister; and I won't *be* married to a minister. Think it over. It's your choice!" Her voice sounded colder than usual.

I couldn't understand it. It was noticeable to all who knew us that as I drew closer to God, my own attitude toward life and others had improved remarkably. Gone were the hostilities and impatience. This only seemed to make Rose angrier.

I gave up the idea of entering the seminary. It seemed foolish to begin a ministry with the probability of a new divorce on my hands. There was, however, no way I could stifle my growing commitment to Jesus Christ. My increasing interest in the Bible was a constant source of irritation to Rose Marie. The sight of my reading the Bible antagonized her to fits of screaming. I would often wait until she was asleep, then secretly slip into the living room to study.

One day I was praying quietly with Lori in her bedroom. Rose Marie had come home from work, slipping in unnoticed through the front door. She suddenly burst into the bedroom and interrupted our prayers.

"I tell you again," she stormed, "if you do this much more, I'll leave you!" She slammed the door on us as we sat there, startled.

I had become increasingly concerned about the atmosphere surrounding Lori during my absence on road tours, but God didn't overlook that problem. Since Rose Marie had decided some time before that Lori should study for a career as a concert pianist, she had engaged a teacher who turned out to be a committed Christian. My wife tolerated the Christian testimony that Mrs. Beck gave with each of Lori's lessons only because she thought she was the best piano teacher in New York. Mrs. Beck came twice a week for Lori's lessons.

"God must have a sense of humor," I thought to myself. "He's using Rose Marie's ambitions for Lori to keep a Christian witness in my house."

Mrs. Beck's lessons with Lori twice a week gave her spiritual food and encouragement and gave me some peace of mind while I was on tour. That, to me, was worth the cost of the piano lessons.

Coleman McDuff had gone to South Bend, Indiana, to hold meetings and again called me to come and give my testimony. The church turned out to be a large one. As I finished speaking, a young "mod" looking couple got up and began to come down the aisle at a brisk clip. The man was well dressed and had stylish razor-cut hair. The girl was beautiful with long blonde hair. I couldn't imagine what they wanted. Perhaps, I thought, they know the pastor and are trying to get down front to greet him at the end of the service.

They came, however, straight down and knelt at the altar. Then other people began to follow them. I had never given an altar call and didn't know what to do. I went to the first couple who had come down and, like a store clerk, said, "May I help you?"

The young man looked up misty-eyed and said, "We recently saw the movie *Marjoe,* about an evangelist fraud, and decided to come to a meeting for a few laughs. But now we want to give our hearts to Jesus."

The pastor asked me to close in prayer. The request scared me. There were so many needs represented at the altar rail. How was I to pray for all of them? What should I say? I didn't know how to close a service. Sheer passion for the Lord was my sole credential, not biblical knowledge or pulpit expertise. What I had to offer was a little Scripture and a lot of life experience.

I began to pray, and suddenly a severe pain stabbed through my side. For a moment I thought I would collapse.

As I prayed, someone in the center of the church shouted that God had healed his cancer—and the pain instantly left me. I was startled by the strange "coincidence."

Little by little the pattern of what God was doing became more clear to me. More and more as I told the story of God's healing of my cancer, I was asked to lay hands on people and pray for their healing. As I prayed, a mental impression of their particular illness dominated my thoughts.

Sometimes while preaching I would receive a "word of knowledge" from God and not mention my impression of the illness. When I didn't call out the illness, pain would attack my own body and would not disappear until I did announce it. Usually, someone in the congregation would say they had felt a healing that corresponded with my pain.

I had to learn not to let one service influence a later one. It became increasingly necessary to pray before each service so my mind would be wiped clean from all impressions that had taken place at the previous one. In one case I actually developed a painful lump in my body that made me suspect the return of my own cancer. When I prayed, a woman claimed a healing from cancer in that area of her body, and the lumps we both had disappeared.

I was scared! God was opening a door to a new form of ministry that I had never anticipated. I was at a crossroads. I could either choose to confine my ministry to speaking about God's healing work, or I could take on this new ministry of healing and its awesome responsibilities. It would certainly be easier to confine myself to speaking, but that might just mean the limiting of God's working in someone else's life.

When I returned to New York, I tried to share my experiences with Rose Marie. She had been hearing about the healings which were happening in response to my ministry and was very disturbed by them. She had not yet come to terms with my own healing.

"I still don't believe in this stuff!" she said emphatically. "It just cannot be."

"What about that night we were both awakened from a sound sleep," I countered, "and then I was healed of cancer. The doctor confirmed it."

A confused look appeared on her face. "I still don't understand it."

"Can you deny the fact that as seriously ill as I was, I was suddenly healed?"

"No," she responded, "something happened all right, but it must have been a chemical change."

"You bet it was!" I answered victoriously.

I looked over at her. Her muscles were tightened as she sat with perfect posture in a wing chair. "One thing bothered me during that whole ordeal," I said to her slowly.

"You've never once acted like you were happy that I was healed, and I still cannot understand why you won't acknowledge God in this. On the contrary, it's almost as if you are angry with Him."

Rose shifted around in her chair as I continued, "I can only say if *you* had been that ill and had been healed, I would have been very grateful. Even though we are sometimes worlds apart, we are still man and wife. I would think you would at least have feelings for me as a human being!"

We sat together in the living room of our New York apartment, quietly reflecting on the events that had taken place. It was a very peaceful setting; the evening sun was pouring through the window. I told her what God seemed to be doing in my life and of the awesome responsibility of it. I was still hoping that somehow she would be supportive, changing her mind once she realized the significance God had played in our lives.

"It means," I told her, "I would have to turn control of my life over to God in a new way. I cannot reject a gift from God that could be used to help people. I owe Him too much."

"I told you before," she responded, her eyes flashing, "and I'll tell you again. If you get too involved in this whole thing, I'm going to leave!"

"You don't understand what's happening!" I exclaimed, frustrated over my inability to convey to her what had happened and what seemed to me to be her illogical response to the working of God. "He has already entrusted me with this gift. I cannot say no."

We continued to talk and disagree. Finally Rose Marie went off to bed. Our differences remained unresolved. I sat in the living room thinking and praying until the sky showed the pink glow of morning.

Austin, Emmett Kelly, Jr., Patricia Nixon, and Pamela Rosaire playing with chimps in the East Room of the White House.

# 21
# Horses and Ordination

The Emmett Kelly, Jr., Circus ran its course. While deciding if I wanted to tackle another area of show business, I stopped in Evansville to visit my mother who was now in delicate health. While I was there, a telephone call came in from the director of The Royal Lipizzan Stallion Show. He had gone to a great deal of trouble to find me. Hearing that I was no longer with Emmett Kelly, he wanted to reach me before I became involved with another show. I always marveled at how fast news travels in show business.

Would I, he wanted to know, be interested in joining The Lipizzan Show as narrator? This show would require the very opposite of my booming, flamboyant circus announcements. With full symphony orchestra, the narration of The Royal Lipizzan Stallions was very sophisticated and low keyed. There were no peddlers in the stands to distract the audience.

I was to join the show in Seattle, Washington. The first part of my flight was cancelled, and all the connecting planes were late, so I arrived only two hours before show time.

I was met at the plane by Jim, the "director of shovel," more commonly referred to as the "pooper scooper."

"Can you possibly give me an idea of how the show runs?" I asked him frantically as we waited for my bags. Not only did he give me ideas; he went through the whole opening speech, telling all about the acts and their order of presentation. He had memorized the entire show.

The moment we arrived at the coliseum I asked to be taken into the stables. I knew the introductions would not be simple ones. They involved the whole bloodline of each horse. I would have to learn to recognize every horse on sight.

Dashing into the stables, I came face to face with . . . forty-two white horses! They could all have been identical twins as far as I was concerned. In spite of my days in the circus, all I knew about horses was that they had a leg in each corner.

"Good heavens!" I exclaimed, "they *all* look alike! How on earth can you tell them apart?"

"Take another look," Chuck, the stable manager, said. "They do look alike at first, but there is something different about each one. All Lipizzan horses are born black and begin to change to white as they grow older, so some will be whiter than others. Now look at this one," he continued. "His feet are a little bigger than the other horses'. His bloodline is Pluto, and the name of his mother was Amena. Pluto Amena. We've nicknamed him Clyde after the Clydesdale horses with the big hooves.

"This one is Favory Slatina III. Note that his face is a little smaller than the others."

I was to learn there were six bloodlines as I memorized each horse and its name. Chuck was able to show me something different and distinctive about every horse. When he had finished, they were no longer just forty-two white horses. Each one was special. Each had a unique trait.

Only thirty minutes before the performance, dressing in my tuxedo, I continued to commit to memory all the information possible as the orchestra members took their places. I do believe if one more piece of information had been jammed into my head, it would have caused a mental hernia.

The lights went down. My heart started to pound as the overture began. This was it!

The orchestra leader took his bow. The curtains opened, and I nervously stepped out, palms sweating. There was applause as I took the microphone. The horses pranced into the arena, and, miraculously, the performance went smoothly—so well, in fact, that I was even quoted with respect in the Seattle newspaper that reviewed us.

After a time I came to be better acquainted with the horses, took dressage riding lessons so I would understand the moves I was announcing, and read books on horse training.

At the age of thirty-nine I had added a new interest and facet to my show business career.

Within a week after we opened in Canada, I flew down to Miami Beach on Friday, August 17, 1973, for the "General Council" of the Assemblies of God fellowship. There, my miniature booklet would be introduced. Ten thousand had been distributed, and I was the guest speaker. The director of the horse show took my place while I fulfilled this previously planned appearance.

I arrived at Convention Center, and Reverend Zimmerman accompanied me to the platform where I sat quietly until I was introduced. Rising on cue, I spoke before 17,000 people, all pastors and their wives. Following my brief talk in Miami Beach, a flood of ministers approached me and invited me to speak at their churches. One of these ministers was the Reverend Leon Cooke.

"I'm close to where you live in New York," he said. "I have a church in Bay Shore, Long Island, and I'd like to arrange a date with you." He gave me his card. "We have something in common," he continued. "I was a professional violinist before entering the ministry, so I know the field of show business."

I smiled to myself. I told him of my commitment with the Lipizzan stallions but gave him an idea of when we would be in the New York area.

"Give me the dates," he said, "and I'll arrange to book you in the area churches."

I needed Christian fellowship and was very much taken with the open friendliness of the Assemblies ministers I had met. I always invited the local Assemblies pastors and their families to be my guests whenever I toured their areas.

Since I was speaking so often in Assemblies churches, the question, "Have you thought of becoming an Assemblies of God minister?" popped up frequently. While traveling with the horse show, I was speaking every Sunday in one of their churches in practically every state in the union. Soon, the question become more pointed: "Since you are speaking mostly in Assemblies churches, it really seems only right that you should join and support our fellowship."

My independent ordination had served its purpose. The only time I used it was when I ministered in a prison or hospital. Yet, what they were asking me did seem to make sense. I knew, however, the events surrounding my first marriage could be a problem.

I finally discussed it with Coleman McDuff while we were in South Bend, Indiana. I told him just enough of my story in ministerial confidence so that he could realize why it was necessary to keep my first marriage a secret.

Later Coleman McDuff called me in New York from his home in Texas. "You know, Brother Austin," he said, "I think the time is ripe for you to apply for papers with the Assemblies."

"Coleman," I reminded him, "what about the Assemblies of God position on those who have had a previous marriage?"

"Doesn't matter," he answered. "That's all under the blood."

I finally wrote a letter to the New York District of the Assemblies located in Syracuse to state my desire to apply for credentials. I mentioned in my letter that I would be in Binghamton with the Lipizzan horses. By coincidence, the district secretary lived there, and I was told to contact him.

I also met other men on the governing board of the district, but I never raised the issue of my first marriage. Later I would realize that by omitting this information from my application form, I had committed the "sin of omission," leaving myself open to all sorts of condemnation in the future.

I was approved to take the examination. They assigned sixty-five short essays for me to complete in just two weeks before the next meeting. At this meeting the New York district members agreed to recognize the credentials I had obtained from the independent church in Texas.

The horse show still demanded a great deal of my time, so I had to study whenever I could. In Hershey, Pennsylvania, I discovered a very good selection of useful books in the public library. Mr. Hershey, founder of the chocolate industry and the town that bears his name, had been a very religious man, and that fact seemed to affect the nature of the library.

After performing in Utica, I drove to Rochester for an early morning television interview, then rushed to the Syracuse Presbyter meeting. I was completing the latter part of the last essay in my car as it was being filled up at the gas station. I met with the New York Presbytery on October 15, 1973, at 9:30 A.M.

First, my essays had to be approved. I passed! Next a written examination. Passed! Now I was taken in to be presented before the presbytery—seventeen stern looking men around a long table. Joseph Flower, the superintendent of the New York district, sat at the end. As I walked in the door, all heads popped around curiously.

"Brother Miles," Reverend Flower asked, "what makes you feel you have a call to the ministry?"

My answer came directly from my heart. "Because I want to do nothing else but prepare a work for HIM. I *must* preach the Gospel. To tell you the truth, I didn't want it. I tried in every way in the world to keep from entering it." I wondered if this honest statement would jeopardize my chances.

"But," I continued with my story, "my relationship with God started with a miracle. Then God healed me of a fatal disease. God has also entrusted me with His healing power. Now, I have no other choice!"

"And why have you come to the Assemblies?"

"I really had not planned to do that either," I said sincerely. "My ministry has been doing very well; I really don't need to be with a denomination." Then I stated with extra emphasis, "But there is *one* thing I *do* need—to have Christian brothers who will uphold me in prayer, and people for whom I can also pray. Most of my speaking engagements have been in Assemblies churches. And, it has been pointed out to me that I should be more supportive to the Assemblies by becoming a part of that fellowship . . . so, here I am."

They put me through a rigorous verbal examination about the Bible, during which they asked to see my present ordination card. They recognized it as "official."

Before the session ended, someone asked, "Brother

Miles, as a Christian, what would you advise someone who wanted to enter show business?"

I'm not sure what sort of an answer my questioner expected, but I replied, "Here's my advice. If you want to be successful in life, there are two steps. First, heed Matthew 6:33—'But seek ye first the kingdom of God, and his righteousness; and all these things shall be added unto you.' Secondly, when success comes, don't believe your own publicity."

One of the members quipped, "I'd like to remind some of our ministers of point two."

They excused me from the room to deliberate about my case. It took less than one minute. They came out, all smiles, and welcomed me to the family. I was told that I would receive my license immediately and be ordained at the council meeting the following May. They were making an exception to the normal two year period between licensing and ordination for me. The examination ended at 9:00 P.M.

When the time came for my ordination seven months later on May 22, 1974, the timing again was perfect. I was with the Lipizzan show in the Midwest but had a day off between shows. I flew to the New York District Council Convention in Utica, New York, for my ordination. Rose Marie, unfailing in her opposition to my ministry, had refused to come. The meeting was well covered by the press. Before going in, a reporter asked me, "Isn't any of your family here?"

I choked back the emotion welling up within me. Taking some comfort in the large crowd going in the doors of the church, I gestured toward them saying, "Take a look. I'd say my family is very well represented here."

The church was packed. Four hundred ministers were present. Lively hymns were being sung. Even though it was only a few minutes before the ceremony, I was ushered quickly into a side room. An anonymous minister asked me to pray for his healing. He had a brain tumor that was very noticeable. The discomfort of it could no longer be controlled by medication. A tight strain was in his eyes.

Along with some other ministers who had gathered, I laid hands on him and prayed. The tumor disappeared!

Everyone in the room began to shout and clap. One jumped up and down. Out front the congregation was singing "Power in the Blood." It was, to me, a most appropriate beginning for this new ordination!

The ceremony began. There was a hush as my name was called. Reverend Joseph Flower asked my intentions; then the charges of the ministry were given me by Reverend R.D.E. Smith. Standing directly in front of me as I knelt at the altar, he read my charges from 2 Timothy 4:1-5.

> **I charge thee therefore before God, and the Lord Jesus Christ, who shall judge the quick and the dead at his appearing and his kingdom; Preach the word; be instant in season, out of season; reprove, rebuke, exhort with all longsuffering and doctrine. For the time will come when they will not endure sound doctrine; but after their own lusts shall they heap to themselves teachers, having itching ears;**
> **And they shall turn away their ears from the truth, and shall be turned unto fables.**
> **But watch thou in all things, endure afflictions, do the work of an evangelist, make full proof of thy ministry.**

"Brother Miles," said Joseph Flower, standing on the platform, "with the authority vested in me as Superintendent of the New York District of the Assemblies of God, I ordain you to the Christian ministry."

He then asked the presbytery to come forward and lay hands on me and offer prayer. "The laying on of hands signifies that you have been 'set apart,' " Reverend Flower continued. At the time, I had no idea just how "apart" I would be set by that particular laying on of hands. Reverend Smith had already written the independent church in Texas to inform them that my credentials with them would no longer be valid since I was coming into their fellowship.

I was now a fully ordained minister of the Assemblies of God.

I was asked to speak after the ordination. Winding up my talk, I said, ". . . There have been many adventures and events in my life, and many rewards. I've had the opportunity to mingle with people in virtually every walk of life. I've known the worst of life, and the best of life. But of all the events, nothing has ever, or could be, more significant to me than this night to be ordained into this great fellowship. This is truly the happiest moment of my life."

Mike Douglas, Austin, and Roger Miller discussing the Lipizzan horses on the "Mike Douglas Show."

# 22
## 'You Are Special'

As The Royal Lipizzan Stallions crisscrossed the nation, I found myself preaching in virtually every state.

In October of 1974 the horse show visited Charlotte, North Carolina, and another door opened. The host pastor of a local church was connected with the PTL (Praise The Lord) television program in Charlotte. I was invited to appear on the program. At that time it was part of Trinity Broadcasting Network. Their telecast beamed from a small studio on Independence Boulevard and was carried over six stations. They were in the early growing stage. Even though they could not afford any payment of travel expenses, my love of the Lord prompted me to go to Charlotte at their request, in advance of my scheduled trip to the area. Many other people also donated their appearances to help Jim Bakker get his work firmly established; one, a vivacious young blonde singer who was on the same show with me. Her name was Evie Tornquist.

Before appearing, I began to reflect on the negative messages I had heard from other preachers, especially those who pound the pulpit and delight in telling people how sinful they are. Knowing it had turned me off from religion, I reasoned it surely must have affected others the same way. When Jim Bakker introduced me, I walked on camera and said, "Jim, I have something to say to you and to everyone watching." I turned directly to the camera, thrust my hand forward and said, "YOU ARE SPECIAL!"

Before Jim could take a breath, I began to spin stories about people who felt unwanted but were able to succeed when they finally realized that they were special—people like the midgets Sonny Riley and June Dewsberry, and my giant friend Eddie Carmel.

I knew as I said the words *you are special* that they would be the emphasis and trademark of my future ministry. It was a thought that had been on my heart but had not been clearly articulated until that moment on TV. I knew from my own experiences and my counseling work that our society was filled with hurting people who needed self-esteem.

The PTL switchboard began to flash wildly. People responded immediately to the "you are special" message. PTL Club rebooked me, and I turned out to be a regular guest at Heritage Village, PTL's headquarters.

The "you are special" emphasis, so joyfully received by many, was stoutly disputed by some others. After an especially blessed service in the Midwest, a visiting preacher came to me with fire in his eyes. He shook angrily as he berated me.

"My brother, you are bound for hell!" he stated. "It is written that in the last days there will be false prophets! With your false doctrine, you are tearing apart all the good work the church is doing."

"Would you mind telling me what this 'false doctrine' is that I'm preaching?" I asked patiently.

"This error that everybody is special," he boomed, madder than ever. "The Bible tells us that we are to be humble," he rattled on. "Now, young man, I'm going to give you a Bible lesson. It is written in Romans 3:23, that we are all sinners and have come short of the glory of God."

"With all respect, my brother," I said, "that Scripture accurately reads, 'For all HAVE sinned, and come short of the glory of God.' Jesus died forgiving us our sins!"

"NO, NO!" he screamed, his voice echoing out the window of the office and into the parking lot. "There is no good in any of us. Not in me, certainly not in you, not in ANYONE. We are ALL sinners. If you don't keep reminding people of that fact, you are freeing them and opening the pathway for them to continue sinning!"

I took a deep breath so as to properly place my voice. "I believe it is just the opposite. Keep telling people they are bad, and they will eventually live up to the reputation you've given them. Look, reverend, I don't believe the church should inflict guilt on people. Sometimes I think this kind of preaching does more harm to the cause of Christ than good. I think it's time somebody came along and told people how good they are for a change."

Losing all control, this visiting "angel unaware" slammed his fist down on the desk to punctuate his reply. "People like you are ruining the church!" he yelled. "Man is an unworthy creature; there is no good in any of us!"

"Are we really that bad?" I asked.

"Vile, despicable!" he shot back.

"Then that sure tears apart a Scripture I believe in," I sighed.

"And which one is that?" he mumbled.

"Where God said, 'Let us create man in our image.' If that's the case, then God must be pretty terrible if His image is what you say it is. If God is that horrible, then I'm getting away from Him as quickly as I can."

His face by now was red, his cheeks puffed with righteous indignation.

"Reverend," I said softly, "what does it mean in Ephesians 2:10 where it is written, 'For we are his workmanship, created in Christ Jesus unto good works, which God hath before ordained that we should walk in them'? I don't know about you," I said with sincerity, "but that makes me and the people to whom I preach feel pretty special. It gives us the incentive to try to be a dwelling place for the Holy Spirit, for which God created us."

"You are perverting Scripture," he accused, shaking harder than ever. I was actually beginning to feel sorry for him as I walked over and held open the door. He left, taking his hell fire and damnation with him.

A steady flow of letters from people representing all walks of life continued to assure me that my "you are special" theme was reaching a vast number of people. Some wrote to me about their depressions and suicide plans when they thought God had made a "mistake" with them. In one city in the West, a well-dressed attractive woman in her early forties insisted on talking to me following the service.

"I just want you to know," she told me, "that I recently reached the breaking point of my life. I decided to kill my-self."

She started to sob quietly as she related the event to me. "I had been up all night. At 5:30 A.M. I flipped on the TV set, and there you were on PTL with your finger pointing right at me saying, 'You are special.' I had never felt that way before. I listened, and what you said changed my whole life. I live a long way from here, but I just had to make the trip to tell you."

Another testimony came in from a midget couple who were so ashamed of their appearance they refused to come out of their house. While watching PTL on their TV, they caught one of the "you are special" messages. Gaining new self-esteem, not only did they come out of their house, but they began to socialize and joined a Bible study group.

There were so many happy testimonies coming to me that I definitely decided not to be deterred in preaching, "You Are Special."

Of course, a full report of my bluntness to the "man of God" who had disagreed with my "you are special" message was received at Springfield headquarters, and I guess the word began to spread that maybe Austin Miles did not necessarily fit into the mold they had cast for Assembly of God ministers.

# 23
# A Unique Chaplaincy

The next two years were among the most varied and interesting in my life as I combined the work of an ordained minister and full-time performer. I held a chapel service each Sunday. We called our worship area the Oasis of Faith Chapel. Usually, services were held in the stable, using a bale of hay as the pulpit.

The publicity from our traveling church naturally attracted some critics from the "establishment." One stern preacher, with a lofty attitude of superiority, came over one day with friends to eye our "church." "This business of preaching in a stable. Isn't it rather undignified?" he queried pompously.

"Brother," I asked, with a twinkle in my eye, "isn't that where the whole thing started?"

By this time I had accepted additional responsibilities from the Department of Chaplaincies of the Assemblies of God as an industrial chaplain and as the first appointed "Chaplain to Show Business."

However, I soon discovered that not all pastors were happy with the idea of the Assemblies of God having an ordained minister still working in show business. That discovery came when The Lipizzan Show was traveling to Niagara Falls, New York, for four days that would include a Sunday. I wrote to an Assemblies pastor there and offered to speak in his church. I enclosed a copy of the little booklet about me and sent a list of churches where I had spoken.

The Pastor answered with this letter.

Dear Mr. Miles:

In answer to your letter offering to speak in my church. Quite frankly, people in THIS part of the country would criticize your ministry if you spoke in church on Sunday morning, and then, took part in 'that' performance in convention hall in the afternoon. I'm sorry!!!

Sincerely yours in Christ,

Pastor Jack Piper.

Pondering this reply, I dropped the pastor's letter in an envelope along with a note from me to Reverend R.D.E. Smith.

Dear Brother Smith:

You will be interested in the enclosed letter from Reverend Piper. It looks like a prophet is not without honor save in his own district. I do hope when Christ comes with HIS white horse, he'll have an easier time getting a congregation in Niagara Falls than I did. I'm going there with 42 of them!

Yours in Him,

Austin.

An entry in my journal during that period shows the extent of my ministry-show business involvement. In one year I narrated 256 Lipizzan shows in 125 cities; preached 109 times in 70 different churches; and appeared on 107 telecasts, 250 radio broadcasts, and gave countless newspaper interviews. I also taped an additional 100 religious TV spots while carrying on full responsibility as chaplain minister to the company, drove 63,000 miles by car, and logged 20,000 miles by plane. On one occasion I set some kind of record for confusion by forgetting what city I left my car in! It was a wearing time.

Occasional emergencies were intermingled into this schedule, and I would dash off to a hospital to visit an injured performer. At times I became so exhausted I wondered which was more important, to eat something or get some sleep.

There were, however, other compensations that helped break the solemnity of this demanding schedule. I was ready to preach to a packed church in Macon, Georgia, and the pastor seemed a little nervous as he introduced me. "We have as our special guest speaker this morning," he stammered, "none other than Austin Miles, who is the narrator of The Royal Lesbian Show."

Increasingly, as knowledge of my chaplain's role became known, I was called on to counsel show business people. While offstage, simple clerical garb with a Roman collar became the symbol of my work and my identification for those who would need my help.

One of the girls in The Lipizzan Show came to me with a problem. She was going back home for the first time to visit her father who was a midget. She needed advice about how to deal with this difficult confrontation and his lack of height.

"Don't judge a man by the size of his body," I said gently, "but by the size of his heart." We prayed together, asking God's wisdom and love to attend this reunion. Later, I found out it was a wonderful experience for both of them. She returned after her holiday, an invigorated person.

Then, the love bug struck The Lipizzan Show. A young couple wanted to be married on horseback, since the horses were a main part of their lives. The "church" was to be Madison Square Garden between performances. I was pleased when they asked me to marry them. Only members of the family and friends were invited, but the press was allowed to come. I, too, was on horseback. When I asked the groom to say "I do," one horse nodded his head yes in unison with its rider; then both horses appeared to kiss at the same time as the bride and groom. It was an unplanned spontaneous gesture, and the event with the photo drew national coverage.

# 24
# The Decision

The knocking at my motel door was insistent. Groggily, I looked at my watch. 3:00 A.M. I fumbled for the lamp switch, turned it on, and stumbled to the door. A member of the sheriff's department first confirmed my identity and then with regret informed me of my mother's death in Indiana. Her pacemaker had failed while she was out to dinner with friends. She had stepped out of their car and directly into heaven. I thanked God that there had been no suffering or pain.

I was awake the rest of the night. The next morning I arrived as usual at the show in the Shreveport Arena. Everyone was surprised to see me. They thought for sure I would not do the show that day. "Don't you know," I said, in my best show business tradition, "that the show must go on? I'm not only doing the matinee today on schedule, but since today's Sunday, we will still have chapel service this morning, and I expect everyone to be there!" Not cancelling chapel service or the show was an important witness to the company.

Immediately after the Sunday performance, I flew to Evansville to preach my mother's funeral myself. What better tribute could I pay her or God? She had gone to be with Jesus, and that made it a time of rejoicing as well as sorrow.

I called Rose Marie to make arrangements for Lori to fly to Indiana. Lori loved her grandmother very much. Rose Marie opposed the suggestion that Lori be present at the funeral, but my emphatic insistence convinced her to put Lori on the next plane.

When I met the plane the night before the funeral, Lori came running toward me. Not far behind was Rose Marie.

I looked at her questioningly.

"Surprise," she said.

As we stood by the casket together, I said to Lori, "Just remember, baby, you're not looking at grandmom. You're looking at the vessel God loaned her for this life. She is with Jesus. There's no question about that!"

She squeezed my hand and said, "Daddy, I'm so glad we're Christians, or I would probably fall apart right now." She was only twelve, but her faith was so strong that it strengthened everyone there.

I was conducting my first funeral service. At the graveside, as I read from Isaiah, four people knelt and gave their hearts to the Lord, two people received the baptism of the Holy Spirit, and a divorced couple were reunited.

Rose and Lori remained in Evansville for a few days while I took a plane back to New Orleans where I had an evening performance to do.

My great disappointment in two marriages was filling me with bitterness. I had read John Wesley's journal and readily identified with him. He obviously was a lonely and frustrated man. I wondered if some of his long evangelistic trips were not taken for the purpose of getting away from his wife. Yet, despite his marital difficulties, Wesley was able to turn his life and energy over to God, and the result was the great revival which brought the Methodist Church into existence.

One entry in Wesley's journal states, "My wife departed from me today. I shall not go and fetch her."

We were in Johnstown, Pennsylvania, when I reached a selfish and irreversible decision—to leave The Lipizzan Show and go into the ministry on a full-time basis. I telephoned Lori and heard her excitedly exclaim, "Oh, daddy, I think it's wonderful!"

After the show in Johnstown, a woman named Grace Nicodem introduced herself. "You don't know me," she said. "The Lord has sent me to tell you that if you should be available for meetings, I will book you in the Pittsburgh area. *My* ministry is to help ministers."

I looked at her in disbelief. "I'm leaving show business in four days to go into the ministry full time!" I related, amazed over God's perfect timing.

A second confirmation of my decision was given to me within the next few minutes. Two friends of mine, Marge and Andy Krehlik, had driven over form Latrobe to visit with me. "We made the trip over to see you," Marge said, "because Andy and I have had a strong feeling that it is time that you stop performing in arenas and start preaching in them."

The four days passed quickly. It was Sunday, the day of the final performance. I wondered how I would narrate my last show. I thought of the many years of dancing, magic, clowning, acting, ringmastering, and the pain and promises that had brought me to this new decision. Show business had been good to me. It had given me some of the most wonderful times of my life, and now I was ready to cut these ties at the age of forty-two.

My meditation was broken by a phone call. It was Grace Nicodem. True to her word, she had already begun to set up meetings. She had arranged to have me speak at the Pittsburgh Charismatic Conference. The conference was to be in that very arena one week later. That afternoon I said my farewell to show business!

I looked at my calendar. The New York District Council of the Assemblies of God was then meeting in Poughkeepsie, New York. I decided to stop by the meeting on my way home and share the news of my decision with my fellow ministers.

Arriving in Poughkeepsie, I bumped into a friend of mine, Leon Cooke, from Long Island.

"I have some great news to share with you," I said excitedly.

"You've left show business," he guessed.

"Yes," I said, a little deflated because of the accuracy of his guess.

"I could see it coming," he said with a smile. "How is Rose Marie taking it?"

"I'll tell you later," I said. "It just happened. I'm on my way home now to tell her!"

Rose Marie did not take it well at all. She cried and sobbed that her life wasn't worth living anymore. I tried to explain to her that my entering the ministry would probably make little difference in *her* life. I would still be "on the road" and would still send money home. The only difference would be that now I would be preaching instead of performing. But Rose Marie was not to be consoled!

# 25
# The Prophecies

The reception I received from the Charismatic Conference in Pittsburgh was a good one. I had faced larger crowds as a performer, but the one in Pittsburgh was the largest I had faced as a minister. Ten thousand people attended.

Following my talk, a young woman in the audience felt led to pray with me. Her prayer took an unusual and dramatic turn—a prophecy was given.

"My son," she began, "I, the Lord thy God, will use you in a mighty way. I have put healing in your hands; yea, in My name will you heal the sick and perform miracles. Yea, my son, you will take this power to distant lands, and they will hear you. You will be confronted by obstacles, but stay true to me, and I, the Lord God, will guide you through to victory."

The young woman was quivering when she finished. It was the first time she had been used in a prophecy, and it was the first one to be given to me! The word *obstacle* seemed to have special emphasis.

Five days later, on May 30, 1976, I spoke at Calvary Temple in Washington, Pennsylvania. This was an independent full gospel church. Following my message Pastor Herb Sweat rushed to the platform and put his hands on me. His hands were quivering as yet another prophecy was given over me. A hush fell over the entire congregation as Reverend Sweat shared the message God had given him concerning me.

"Yea, I am preparing you for a world-wide ministry. Yea, I will lift you to great heights; the world will see you perform great miracles and healings in My name. But, yea, the enemy will be greatly angered, and he will try to discourage you. Yea, Satan will bring calamity upon you and will strike at you from the east, the west, the north, and the south. Yea, you will not only be in the lion's den, but in the very mouth of the lion, and My hand will reach down and pull you from the jaws of that lion and lift you to greater heights than ever before, if you will remain true to Me. Thus saith the Lord!"

The congregation burst out in an emotional response. It took Reverend Sweat a few moments to focus back to those around him. "I . . . I've never had a prophecy like that," Reverend Sweat said, seemingly searching his own mind for the serious significance of what had been revealed to him.

I was bewildered! This was the second prophecy given over me within five days. Both stressed that God would mightily use me, and, on the other hand, both seemed to say, "Be prepared, the going will get rough."

My ministry was widely accepted, and within a short time, I was booked ahead two years. My relationships with the clergy could not have been better. I had moved immediately from being a busy over-booked showman to being a busy over-booked traveling evangelist. But there was a new happiness in my life. I could now make more time for prayer and Bible study.

My first series of meetings, lasting Sunday through Friday, was held in Fulton, New York. "Dear God," I prayed silently, "I would rather You take my life than for me to hinder Your cause in any way. Guide me with Your Holy Spirit."

I took no part of this dedication lightly. To me it was a serious responsibility.

Every service had a special impact of its own as crowds grew and people were healed and spiritually renewed. The host pastor, Dan Raught, and I spent many pleasurable hours together. During the week I had the opportunity to give special ministry to his wife, daughter, and son. I was to see and visit him several times in the future.

As I traveled the evangelistic circuit, I began to gain an insight into a whole new lifestyle, and the new kinds of challenges it presented. One of the horrors of traveling the evangelistic circuit is to hear the words of the pastor saying, "You'll be staying right here in the parsonage with us!"

Freedom of thought and movement was abolished by such an arrangement. The day always started early as the kids were sent off to school at 7:00 A.M. If there was a Christian school, it meant being granted the privilege of conducting morning chapel service in it. Some pastors wouldn't even go to the laundromat without me. Eventually, I made it a rule that the church would provide a motel room for my stay.

There were also small practical things I learned about being a visiting speaker. I once realized after I had mounted the platform that I had drunk too much coffee before the service. During the singing I looked for a way to exit quietly. There was none! I was facing the delivery of a one hour sermon. I began to pray on the matter. The concentration of my prayer was interrupted by the song leader, who boomed loudly, "Let's all turn in our hymnals and raise our voices to sing 'There Is a Living River Flowing Deep Within'!"

One evening, while holding a service in the home of Colonel Trevor Bale, the former ringmaster and head animal trainer with the Ringling Brothers Circus, I told the attentive congregation of thirteen how Christ could work in their lives. They seemed genuinely touched by the service. Afterward, one of the women stopped me and said, "You know, my daughter has never been christened. Could you do that?"

"I certainly could," I responded. "We can do it right now."

"My daughter hasn't been christened either," another woman chimed in.

Although christening is not a term used in the Assemblies of God, it didn't seem necessary to quibble about terminology. I was sure I could provide a dedication service that would coincide with their understanding of christening.

Within fifteen minutes, the mothers were back with their daughters. The two girls were in white dresses, and their hair had been combed and fixed up for the occasion. This was a serious spiritual occasion for the families. We gathered at the home-made altar, and using a borrowed sterling silver cup, I sprinkled the children with distilled water and dedicated them to the Lord.

At the conclusion of the service, Colonel Bale approached

me. "Reverend Miles," he said, "there is something I'd like you to do. It would mean a lot to all of us. We have a tiger cub named Madrass. He's going to be a very special tiger, and we'd like to have a special blessing on him. Would you christen Madrass for us? It would mean so much."

Pondering for a moment, I could see the genuine sincerity of these people. "O.K.," I decided, "BRING ME THE TIGER!"

A beautiful, snarling little tiger cub was placed in my arms. "It is written in Genesis," I recited, "that 'God created the beasts of the earth each after his kind.' Since God created the beasts, we should treat our animal friends with kindness, never causing them unnecessary pain. Since this is going to be a special beast working in harmony with man to bring joy to others, it's our hope that somehow through this unique partnership, a Christian testimony can evolve. With that in mind, I hereby dedicate you, Madrass Tiger, in the name of the Father, the Son, and the Holy Spirit. Amen."

Madrass is perhaps the only tiger in or out of captivity that has a "certificate of dedication" to God.

Austin and Hercules studying Scripture together at the home of Ron and Joy Holiday in St. Petersburg, Florida.

# 26
# Bless This Mess

While traveling for the Lord, I began to feel an increasing sense of inward peace. As I visited the homes of the various pastors, however, I wondered why I did not have the same love and family life they enjoyed.

Back in New York, Rose Marie was pushing Lori toward a career as a concert pianist. Lori was performing superbly and winning awards for her piano artistry, but she was not happy with the prospect of being a concert pianist. She told me about the frustrations of competing with students whose whole world revolved around a grand piano. Lori had no such obsessive commitment to a concert career and had become tense and depressed. Nevertheless, Rose Marie took her out of private school and enrolled her in the High School for Performing Arts in New York City.

I was not enthusiastic about the change. Performing Arts was a high pressure school. Students were admitted only after satisfactory auditions in their areas of specialty. Each year some 4,000 hopefuls competed for approximately 225 openings.

However, God again showed His providential care when Lori called from school one day. "Daddy," she bubbled excitedly, "there are eleven born-again Christians in this high school!" That statement made my day.

When I returned home for a visit before leaving on a crusade to Savannah, Georgia, Rose seemed much more relaxed than she had been previously. The visit home had been a delight. Things were not only peaceful, but enjoyable.

"You know, Rose," I said, putting my arm around her waist, "I just knew that things would work out between us.

There's been a lot of rough spots, but it looks like we are finally going to make it."

"Yes, I guess that's true," she said softly.

I felt genuine happiness flood through me as I thought of the coming holiday season. Christmas was less than a month away. The decorations were already up in New York. It was 1976 and the first time in three years that I would be free to enjoy being in my apartment with my family.

"I've learned a lot of things in my ministry," I said to her tenderly. "One thing is how to be a little more understanding. From now on we're going to have a happy marriage."

The services in Savannah were to begin on November 28. I had to leave a day early. Rose agreed to drive me to the airport. As we went down into the parking garage to get the car, she seemed happy.

"Here, you drive," she said, smiling as she handed the keys to me.

We parked in front of the terminal, and Rose stayed with the car while I took my bags in; then I came back out to where she was standing. My preaching engagements would end on December 5.

"Can we put the tree up early this year?" I asked.

"Yes, that we can do," she said agreeably.

"Do you think you could have it up when I get back by the fifth?" I asked hopefully. "I'd like to have it up for the whole month and just keep December open as our family month."

"Yes, sweetheart, the tree will be up when you return," she assured me. She kissed me goodbye warmly. It was the most affectionate send-off she had ever given me.

The airplane ran into a dense fog, and we were forced to land in St. Louis, Missouri. I called home during our wait. Rose sounded highly nervous and anxious to conclude the call.

The fog did not lift, and the Atlanta airport was completely socked in. It looked doubtful that I would be able to reach my destination in Savannah that night. Once again I telephoned my home from St. Louis. This time I spoke to

Lori and asked her to contact the pastor in Savannah to tell him about my delay. She, too, seemed strangely uncommunicative.

In Atlanta on Wednesday evening, I called home before the church service. There was no answer. After the service, despite the late hour, I tried again. Again, no answer. After midnight I began to worry and tried phoning every fifteen minutes until early in the morning.

The next day a letter came just before the service. Rose Marie wrote that it was all over! She and Lori had moved out, and she was filing for divorce. The pastor could see by my expression that the letter contained bad news. I shared the situation with him, asking him not to say anything about it. Then I asked him to please pray that God would supply me with extra strength for the evening service.

Instead of the sermon I had planned, I preached that night on love. God richly blessed the service, but after it was over, I was unable to eat or sleep, and I was sick most of the night. It was the same all day Thursday. Although I delivered strenuous sermons Thursday and Friday nights, I still could not sleep.

On Saturday, just a week after I had left New York, I returned to my apartment. Hesitating before putting the key into the lock, I wondered what I would find inside. The apartment had been beautiful and elegant, furnished with antiques from all over the world.

Slowly, I opened the door. The first thing that came into focus was a poster that Rose Marie had put up to greet me. It said, "Keep Smiling." The furniture was gone. Travel posters replaced the original oil paintings and other valuable art objects. The message of total rejection was unmistakable. I still couldn't seem to grasp the finality of the situation. After I had opened and shut the door, my neighbor opened his door.

"I thought you moved," he said curiously.

"No," I replied slowly, "my wife and daughter moved."

He told me that the furniture had been moved out the Saturday before, the moment we left for the airport.

Filled with depression and loneliness, I wandered out

onto the street. "Why, Lord, why?" I asked over and over. I wondered why God had brought me this far to be crushed so completely. It was snowing. Brightly colored, flickering Christmas lights glowed through the windows of the homes I passed in Forest Hills.

"Lori must have been in on the plot all along," I thought agonizingly. The move was made during the time I called from the airport. Lori hadn't given me any indication that they were leaving. Where was she? Why did she leave? There were so many unanswered questions!

I wandered aimlessly in the snow. Suddenly, I came face to face with Father Johnson. I told him what had happened. He tried to have me come to the rectory with him. I declined. I just wanted to walk for awhile. "I am here, available to you at any time. Please call me," he offered sympathetically.

Much later, wet with snow, I returned to the apartment. I had never been free to pray or praise God unhindered in this place. For the first time I walked into each room and praised God out loud. It was good to hear the word *God* echo off the bare walls.

That evening I was up all night pacing through the empty rooms. I couldn't bear the thought of spending Christmas in New York alone! However, I had a commitment to preach in Stanley Berg's church in New York that afternoon and evening.

Reverend R.D.E. Smith, who by now had been elevated to the position of a national presbyter, flew in, and he and Reverend Berg asked for a meeting with me. I had now been served with papers from Rose Marie. They asked how this would affect my ministry. I told them I intended to continue as usual. This seemed to satisfy their concern.

Since December was free and I couldn't locate my daughter, I decided to make a trip to the Assemblies of God evangelists' seminar in Springfield, Missouri. I flew out, hoping to find a little fellowship and encouragement from the "brotherhood."

Reverend Thomas Zimmerman made a special point to assure me that all the ministers were praying for me during this difficult trial. Then I spoke to Reverend Paul Markstrom, the director of the department of chaplaincies.

"I feel no anger toward Rose Marie," I told him.

Reverend Markstrom said, "That's not normal. You should allow yourself to be angry, let it out, don't keep it bottled up within you. It's not healthy!"

I was surprised at this statement.

"What are your plans?" he asked.

"To continue with the ministry God has given me. It looks like I'll have to go it alone, but I've been alone most of the time anyway." I shrugged my shoulders, resigned to my fate.

Meanwhile, requests came in for my preaching services over the holiday period. Reverend Leon Cooke called me from Bay Shore, Long Island. "Something urgent has come up," he said, "and I must be out of town over Christmas. Could you please take my church the day after Christmas, the twenty-sixth? I really need your help!"

I agreed to do the services for him.

Five days before Christmas, Lori called. "Hello, daddy," she said with uncertainty in her voice. "How do you feel?"

"How do you think I feel after all this?" I asked. We spoke of other things; then she began to cry and hung up.

I discovered that Rose Marie was planning to take Lori out of the country. I called my lawyer, and he immediately put a freeze on Lori's passport, requiring Rose Marie to bring the passport to his office.

She was livid with rage as she screamed at me over the phone, "I'll fix you! I'm going to expose you to the church. I'll tell them everything about your past life!"

Lori called again. This time she told me flatly that she never wanted to see me again. I had written in my journal that "never again will I shed tears over any female"; yet, after hearing my own daughter say she wanted nothing more to do with me, I cried uncontrollably.

Two days before Christmas Lori called and said she wanted to see me. We met in Manhattan on Fifth Avenue and went to a little French restaurant. A big lighted Christmas tree was near the entrance, and lights and holly were strung all about. Lori was tense and nervous, stiff and proper, all defenses up.

"First of all, baby, I'm not angry with you for what happened," I assured her. "You're my daughter, and I love you more than anyone. My door will always be open anytime you want to come to see me. As for Rose Marie, I want you to tell her something."

Lori stiffened up, feeling that she was about to be caught in the middle of a battle. Her face relaxed as I continued.

"Tell her I'm sorry for whatever I did that caused her to take this drastic action."

After we finished our meal, I walked with her to the subway. "Let's stop in this store for a moment," I said to her. I bought a present for Rose and had it gift wrapped.

"Give it to her, and tell her I sincerely wish her a merry Christmas."

Before she left, I asked Lori to please not let Jesus out of her life. I also asked her to have Rose call me. "Tell her I have no animosity toward her, but I want to spend some part of Christmas with you."

We parted on a friendly note, with Lori giving me a light peck on the cheek.

"What is this business of you wanting Lori during Christmas?" Rose Marie screamed at me over the phone.

"I am her father," I said, "and that certainly is not asking too much!"

"And what am I supposed to do? Be by myself on Christmas?"

Finally it was agreed that Rose Marie would have Lori on Christmas eve, and I would have her on Christmas afternoon.

I still had to face Christmas eve alone—a day when families are making their preparations for the holiday. All around me were signs of Christmas joy, but I was deeply depressed.

Then I began to realize how selfish I was being. "What's wrong with me?" I thought. "If I'm depressed with Christ in my heart, how awful it must be for those who do not have Jesus. They have to face this season without Him." Then I asked, "Lord, what do I have to share?"

I thought about the Bibles I had from the American Bible Society to use in my work as a chaplain. I bought some

Christmas paper, wrapped each Bible, and then put them in shopping bags. In my clerical suit, with the shopping bags over my arms, I headed out into the early evening. I learned that broken hearted people are very easy to find.

Getting off the subway near Bryant Park, I encountered a bearded man walking alone with a slow, heavy step. I said, "Hey, brother, Merry Christmas in the name of the Lord! Here's a present for you."

He stopped and looked at me with sorrow. Tears welled up as he grabbed my hand and shook it so warmly that I thought it would fall off. We began to talk about God. Life had fallen apart for him, and he had been considering suicide. The holiday season with all its surrounding gaiety is a most treacherous time for anyone with a heavy heart.

I gave one Bible to a woman whose clothes were obviously not adequate for the cold, but the gesture did seem to brighten the sadness that had been on her face.

After giving away several Bibles, I decided to go to Luchow's for dinner. It would be nice to see their Christmas tree, which has become a New York tradition. Luchow's usually requires advance reservations. I decided to take my chances. I told the maitre d' that I didn't have a reservation.

"You, chaplain," he interrupted, "don't need a reservation." I was taken to the best table near the tree. The head violinist recognized me and came over to chat. Several patrons in the restaurant made a special effort to come to my table and wish me holiday greetings. Many times in New York no one recognized me. But on that night God knew how badly I needed human contact. Everywhere I went people called me by name. Some had seen me on the Joe Franklin TV show in New York or on PTL; others knew me from show business.

I headed next to Sloane Kettering Memorial Hospital to visit some cancer patients. They, too, were alone this Christmas eve! Sharing with them made my burden easier to bear and lifted my spirits.

It was now very late. I had a growing desire to attend the famous Midnight Mass at St. Patrick's Cathedral. Tickets for this event were obtained months in advance. Signs on all doors, including the Diocesan office, declared that there were no more tickets available.

"I am a protestant chaplain," I said to the man at the desk. "Is there any way you could slip me in? I'll be glad to stand in the back. It would mean so much to me."

"Every ticket has been given out; we've even had to turn away some dignitaries who wanted to come . . . but for YOU, chaplain," he said with a sudden twinkle in his eye. He vanished into a side office. He came back with an envelope. "Here's the best seat in the house!"

I was ushered in, down the long aisle to one of the front "dignitary pews."

Bishop Fulton Sheen delivered the message. He pointed out that there were really two Christmases–first when Christ was born on earth and secondly when He is born within us.

It was an uplifting message that I shall never forget. In the subway I found a couple holding hands and crying. I learned they had just returned from identifying the body of a family member at the morgue. I gave them a Bible and wished them God's blessings.

When the subway train stopped in Forest Hills, a black motorman leaned out the window. I was sure there were many things he would rather be doing than running a subway train on Christmas eve at 3:00 A.M.

"Merry Christmas in the name of the Lord," I said as I left the train and handed him my last gaily wrapped Bible.

His face brightened, and he took off his glove and shook my hand. As the train disappeared down the track, he was still waving out the window, a big smile dominating his face.

The apartment didn't seem nearly as empty as before. As I knelt beside the bed, I said, "Well, devil, you lost that one. Thank you, Jesus for one of the best Christmas eves I've ever had!"

Lori and I spent a quiet Christmas day together. We had dinner at the home of Reverend and Mrs. Stanley Berg of Glad Tidings Tabernacle. Rose Marie, in the meantime, decided to fly off to Europe alone, leaving Lori to accompany me to the New Year's services I was conducting in Poughkeepsie.

There, she had an opportunity to observe other Christian families.

"Daddy," she finally said to me following the service, "I want to go to church regularly and be in Christian surroundings." She looked into space. "Mommy said if I ever decided to live with you, she would never see me again. She said we'd be finished and then I'd have nobody to look after me. It was my choice—her or you!"

"Well, baby," I said, "it's whatever you decide. If you feel better living with Rose, you have my blessing. You have the keys to my apartment and can come visit me anytime you want."

Shortly after Rose Marie returned, Lori called me. "Dad," she cried, "Mommy and I had a big argument because I wanted to see you and go to church. She said she was going to put me out on the street."

"Nobody's ever going to put you out on the street!" I declared emphatically. "Come on home!"

She came immediately. "Now, Lori," I explained, "I have a heavily booked road schedule of evangelistic services. I'll cut them down so I can spend more time with you in New York while you finish school. I'll call Reverend Berg at the church and see if he knows of a woman there who can stay with you while I'm away. I'll rearrange my schedule in the meantime."

Rose Marie's voice over the telephone screeched in a nonstop barrage of piercing, ear-splitting tones. "I've warned you," Rose Marie stated menacingly, "I DON'T CARE WHAT IT TAKES TO DO IT! I'm going to *ruin* your ministry!"

Lori and I set out to rebuild our home. The first thing we bought was an elegant little plaque for the wall that said "Bless this Mess," and we started out fresh all over again.

The year ahead was to be the most eventful year of my life as I learned to expect the unexpected. I had no clues as to what was going to happen. All I could see was a calendar totally filled with speaking engagements in churches.

During long talks with my daughter, I learned that prior to her leaving, Rose had told Lori of the complications arising from my first marriage, and, attempting to convince her that I was some sort of criminal, she had shown Lori the documents which we both had altered to effect my name change.

I had desperately wanted to protect Lori from the past, but now at the age of fourteen, in view of the latest circumstances, she had to be told the truth. It was very difficult for both of us, but Lori absorbed the information with an unusual calm and serenity.

Lori at age ten practicing to become a concert pianist.

# 27
# 'God Does Not Heal'

The note in my hotel box read, "The pastor will pick you up at 6:30 tonight."

Upon his arrival I noticed he was a good-looking man, about forty, wearing a gray striped suit that exhibited expensive taste. As we drove to the church, he said, "Now, tonight, I don't want you to talk about Divine healing or dwell on Christ. I've been doing that all week. I want you to talk about celebrities. That's what the people want to hear."

His words unsettled me. "You flew me all the way out here for that reason?" I asked. "I left show business to preach the Gospel, and I understood you wanted me to give my testimony, which is a healing testimony and does exalt Christ!"

"Well," he agreed, "maybe you should mention something about it, but don't dwell on it. Whatever you do, wind up your message with a salvation appeal. This is a salvation church. I can preach on Hershey bars, and people will come to the altar to be saved!"

Not believing my own ears, I said quietly, "I would like to hear your sermon on Hershey bars!" We rode the rest of the way in stony silence.

When we arrived at the church, the parking lot was already overflowing. It appeared that the large auditorium would not hold all those who wanted to come.

"Look at that crowd!" the pastor exclaimed with delight. "This is the best Sunday night attendance we have ever had!"

As we walked through the corridor of the church, one of his six staff pastors ran up excitedly. "Look at this crowd! This is the greatest crowd we've ever had!"

I tried to find at least one pastor on the staff who would stop long enough to have prayer with me before approaching the platform, but they were all too busy running around congratulating themselves on the turnout.

As the hour approached, the pastor finally appeared. "Come," he beckoned as he walked me to the rear aisle where we were to make a grand entrance, show biz style. I got my first look at the inside of this enormous church. The place was alive with people. There was an air of great expectancy as the lights dimmed.

"All right," stated the pastor with authority, "as soon as I give you the signal, just after the choir begins, walk alongside me down the aisle to the platform. Then stand before the seat on the right and *wait* for me before you sit down."

As the choir started with "Here Comes the King," the spotlights hit us, and we started our grand entrance. The audience was all keyed up to applaud as we entered. The atmosphere was such that when we got to the platform, I started to reach for my straw hat and cane, feeling I was back in the theatre. All the lights were off, save for a single spotlight shining down on the pastor, who was now at the pulpit.

"People all over the world are watching this church," he boasted. "This is the biggest, fastest growing church in the world, and I am flying to Canada tomorrow to teach a pastor's school on church growth."

"Where does Christ fit into all this?" I wondered, as I watched this circus-like presentation that seemed to exclude the One we were supposed to exalt.

The collection appeal was extremely strong, and the people generously responded to help the church meet the "extra special expenses of bringing in our guest speaker."

When I was finally introduced, there was an enthusiastic response as I began with some quips and stories about what God was doing in New York. As I went into my testimony of healing, a hush fell over the congregation. At the conclusion, the Holy Spirit began to move in a beautiful way, and healings took place all over the auditorium. Then, remembering the pastor's demand, I cut the healing service quite short and made an altar call. People came from all directions to the front, falling on their knees at the altar.

The pastor, furious, came and yanked the microphone out of my hand. "How many of you felt you were touched at this service?" he fairly yelled into the mike. Hands were raised all over the auditorium.

"I mean," he continued defiantly, "how many of you *actually* feel that God *healed* you during this service?" More hands lifted, and several stood wanting to testify.

More annoyed than ever, the pastor quickly addressed the ones kneeling at the altar, then the confused new 'converts' were hustled off to a side room where they were urged to sign membership cards and tithe pledges.

This affair concluded, the pastor hurried off the platform to his office. Before I could get away, I was surrounded and swept up by a sea of people wanting to talk, shake hands, and ask for extra prayer. Some were talking about the free fishing trips to Canada offered as being an incentive to join the church. It was quite awhile before a strange man finally came to me and said, "I will drive you back to your motel."

"What about the pastor?" I asked.

"He's in his office."

"My coat is there," I said. "I'll go get it and say goodnight to him."

When I entered the room, the pastor was sitting at his desk, writing.

"I've just written you a note," he said as he rose to his feet. "Do you want to see it?"

"Sure," I answered.

He thrust his hand-written note at me, then began to pace back and forth in the room. I looked at him, then read the note he had shoved into my hand.

Bro. Miles:

Just a brief word of my utter disappointment in your ministry tonight. I feel that one of the first obligations of a guest is to be submissive to the host pastor. This church is not full by accident, but by design and God's rich blessing. I want you to know "the positive confession" does *not* hold up in totality of all of God's Word. Also, one of our faculty members has M.S. Where were the results for her? I trust you will be more submissive to future pastors.

It was signed, and I noticed that he had capitalized most of his words. He spun around to face me with such intensity that I expected to have to defend myself from physical attack.

"You have caused confusion in my church! You have ruined my church . . . ," he charged, jamming a finger at me.

"I don't believe you will find I've hurt your church," I answered softly. "I think you will find just the contrary."

"Where do you come off with this business of God healing people?" He was now furiously pounding his desk.

"I come off with it because it is in the Bible and stated for *now*," I replied earnestly.

Anger swept over his face. "I know the Bible inside and out. God does NOT heal people!" he screamed, hammering his desk with his fist more fervently than ever. "The book of Job proved that, and Paul's thorn in the flesh was never removed," he declared emphatically, pounding the desk in rhythm to his words, trying to accent each one with a thump!

"This is an Assemblies of God church, isn't it?" I asked as my own indignation mounted.

"That's right, and one of the biggest!" he bragged again.

"And you are an Assemblies of God minister?" I asked with disbelief.

"That's right, for many years."

"And you don't believe in Divine healing, or even positive faith???" I was flabbergasted!

"There is no such thing!" he retorted.

My mind was now spinning. The doctrine of the Assemblies of God stresses faith and Divine healing. How could anyone not believing this still be an Assemblies minister? The statement of doctrine must be answered every year when the minister's credentials are renewed and he fills out a new application. All of the pastors I had met previously openly professed their belief in positive faith and Divine healing. I stared at him in amazement.

"God does *not* heal people," he insisted again.

"I'm sure glad you told me, brother," I said, recovering from my bewilderment. "Otherwise, I would only *believe* I was well!"

"I can't believe this," I continued with exasperation. "You have no faith . . . and yet you're remaining a minister?"

"I'll just tell you this," he screamed hysterically, not answering my question. "For what you did I will ruin your ministry! I am powerful and respected, and when I pass the word, your ministry will be finished!" Rather than intimidate, his threats only served to infuriate me.

"Before you get too carried away, my dear brother, I suggest we play the tape of this service to your district, and then in Springfield, and see if they feel I am wrong in my doctrine. In fact, all of my sermons are on tape, and I am preaching the same thing I have preached from the beginning. If you wish, we will *both* go to Springfield headquarters, and if they tell me I'm wrong, then the whole doctrine of the Assemblies of God fellowship will have to be changed!"

The discussion continued, even more heatedly, as my voice projected over his.

"I just cannot believe this," I reiterated. "You have been a preacher all this time, and yet you honestly have no faith that God has power today? What you are telling your congregation, pastor, is that 'God is dead, so let's just gather together for a history lesson, and I'll be your advisor.' " By now I was pounding the desk also. "This isn't a church; this is a country club!"

My temper and indignation exploded, forcefully. "If you are not giving the people faith to hold onto, then what ARE you giving them for their tithes, pastor? No, on second thought, don't tell me, I know–free fishing trips to Canada . . . and you're traveling around the world conducting 'pastor' schools??? This is incredible! You are misleading other ministers into thinking that success is measured by the number of people in the church, no matter what means are necessary to get them in. You may think you have it made, that you're on solid rock, but are you in for a rude awakening! You, reverend, are on sinking sand!

"Most people go to church hoping for a spiritual uplift. What on earth do you have to offer people to increase their spirituality? The privilege of giving you their tithes and going on a fishing trip once a year? You would never have reached *me* with that gimmick! The only thing that changed me was the positive faith I saw in action. If you can't give the people faith—you're giving them nothing! Thank God I have been a part of so many miracles that someone like you could never turn me off! God is still here today, and the same healing power is available today as it was when Jesus walked the earth."

"What about that faculty member of mine with M.S.?" the Pastor demanded arrogantly. "I've prayed for her, and nothing happened!"

"*That's* it!" I exclaimed, now beginning to understand his problem. "Because your prayer was not answered to suit you, you refuse to recognize that God will heal anyone and that others are given this gift. I believe, sir, had God honored your prayer, you would then have tried to walk on water! You would have taken personal credit for the healing, and Christ would not have been exalted!

His jaw dropped open as if he had been struck with a club.

"I'm telling you, brother," I said now lowering my voice, "you'd better get on your knees and seek God's will in your life and for this church, or you are going to fall hard. And, what's worse, when you do, a lot of innocent people are going to fall with you, and their blood will be on your hands. Your punishment will be the most severe of all!"

The pastor's eyes suddenly dropped, and his words cracked as he feebly rationalized. "Maybe it's my Baptist background that is getting in my way."

"No, it's not that, my brother," I said softly, "it is ego—pure ego. You had better start building a monument to Christ instead of to yourself."

"Maybe it's good that we had this talk," he said, regaining his composure. "Come on; I will drive you back to your motel."

When he dropped me off at the motel, he handed me an envelope.

"If you really feel I've hindered your work, then keep it. You don't owe me anything," I said.

"No," he insisted, "it would not be Christian not to pay you for coming."

I accepted, said goodbye, and went to my room. When I opened the envelope, I found the check did not even cover my travel expenses.

The next day in New York I walked the streets for three hours. "Lord, are You sure I am supposed to be in the ministry?" I kept asking. Thinking about the circus, show business, even the world itself as I walked, I seemed to hear an invisible symphony playing a medley of "Amazing Grace" followed by "March of the Gladiators."

One week later, a short note arrived from the pastor.

> I just wanted you to know that last Sunday we reached the same peak attendance *without* a guest speaker as we did when you were here.

I smiled. Inadvertently he was admitting that my ministry had indeed helped his church, not hurt it. I replied as follows:

> Dear Brother –,
>
> Just a note to express my appreciation for being able to minister to your people. There was a good witness of the Spirit on all sides, and I believe you will continue to hear good reports of good things that the Lord did that evening. I was so glad to hear that your attendance continues on an upswing. Even though we are many times different from one another in the ways we approach our ministries, it is beautiful to know that the Lord honors the diversity of gifts of the Spirit, and, praise God, He has made us all individuals.
>
> If you are ever in the New York area, I would

sincerely invite you to let me know and set aside some time for fellowship, during which time you will be my guest. I believe God has honored both of these ministries and will do so in an even mightier way as we draw closer to Him. And, too, my brother, I believe indeed that we could wind up being very good friends and true brothers in Christ if given half a chance. My heart is so open.

May the Lord's hand be upon you. 1 Thess. 1:5.

Ready in His service,

Rev. Austin Miles

Show Business Chaplain
New York City

The Pastor must have been surprised by my response. I received a friendly reply from him. After starting with the usual platitudes, he wrote:

I accept your invitation of hospitality when I am in the New York area. That is very kind of you, and I have every confidence that we would have a very compatible and beautiful experience of Christian fellowship.

In spite of our differing view on methodology, I must tell you that since I have been pastor in this church, I do not know of any service *where more people were healed by the power of God!* We have had testimonies in Pastor's Bible Class; people have voluntarily come to me and have shared how the Lord touched them that night. Now, I have to be honest about this and recognize the miracles of our Lord. I praise God for that. I thought you would like to know this.

May our Lord smile upon all of our efforts for Him. I pray God's blessing upon you and yours.

A month later I was surprised to receive in the mail one

of his church bulletins. It read: Seminar on Healing, starts Wednesday. Points listed were, "Problems in Prayer for the sick; Pointers for Prayer, or Hints for Healing; Power in Prayer for the sick; Popular Approaches to Divine Health." (All to be taught by the pastor, and only two months after he had stated that God did not heal.)

I was amazed that our "argument" had produced such a beautiful new spiritual awakening!

# 28
# The Curse

Jack Anderson's column telling of the Reverend Thomas Zimmerman and his involvement in a banking scandal hit every newspaper in the country. Many of us reacted with shock and disbelief.

The news stories stated that while Reverend Zimmerman was enthroned as grand master of the Assemblies of God Church, he was also the chairman of the board of a Springfield bank. All the millions of dollars being collected worldwide for the Assemblies was sent to Springfield and deposited in this bank. By doing this, Reverend Zimmerman, it was alleged, was able to make personal loans for very little, if any, interest. The particular loan that was brought to the public's attention was for a large sum of money with which the Reverend Zimmerman planned to buy a large commercial tract of land upon which he would build a shopping center.

Like most of us in the church, I was convinced this publicity was a deliberate design to destroy God's work. Surely there was another side to this story.

While I was preaching in Plant City, Florida, Reverend E.R. Schulz, the district secretary, made a special trip to the church to officially welcome me to Florida on behalf of the district. Reverend Schulz was a longtime personal friend of Reverend Zimmerman, and we discussed the matter at length after the service.

"How's Brother Zimmerman taking this?" I asked.

"I can only tell you this," Reverend Schulz answered sadly. "Reverend Zimmerman is a broken man. He just mopes around. He seems to have lost all of his energy. We're all worried about the effect of this upon his health."

"What a pity," I thought. Here was a man who was so dynamic, a powerful leader of charismatics all over the world, who could command an audience of thousands, now beaten down, broken. Something must be done.

"Reverend Schulz," I said, "I think I know how to help. I have met with Jack Anderson in the past. He's an honorable man; in fact, he helped me tremendously during a dark period of my life. Would you get in touch with Brother Zimmerman and tell him I will personally contact Jack Anderson and request an additional investigation be made so that this entire matter can be straightened out."

Then I called Reverend Paul Markstrom in Springfield, knowing that he was very close to Zimmerman, and offered my help. I also dropped Reverend Zimmerman a personal note of encouragement, which I felt he needed.

I was quite surprised to learn that my offer of help was refused.

Meanwhile, I continued to preach, and God's Holy Spirit continued to sharpen my "word of knowledge."

In Reverend Leon Cooke's church in Bay Shore, Long Island, during an evening service, the Holy Spirit revealed that someone had been injured by a gun and suffered severe pains in the leg. A man rushed up to the microphone, openly weeping. He was a New York City detective, who, eleven months before, had been shot in the leg.

"The pain instantly left my leg!" he related between sobs. His wife verified many weeks later that the healing was permanent, and this event was written up in the *New York Beacon,* the district newspaper of the Assemblies.

The auditorium of the Faith Assembly of God Church in Poughkeepsie, New York, was filled to its capacity. The Holy Spirit revealed that there was someone visiting the church who hated policemen, and this hatred was so intense that it could bring about great destruction. I offered prayer that the burden of hate would be lifted.

"Where are you?" I asked as I looked around. There was silence for a minute. Then a voice came from the balcony.

"I'm up here, Reverend Miles," said a young man. "Yes, that was me. I don't live around here. I don't even know why

I came to this church. I had a run-in with the cops some time ago, and I made this trip for one reason—so I could kill a cop. But now . . . ," he cried, "I don't feel that hatred anymore. I feel free!"

Several policemen who were members of the church went to the distraught man and lovingly put their arms around him. This emotional healing was documented by witnesses and inserted in a church magazine.

My daughter also seemed to receive a special touch from God. In one church, through her prayers every young person there received the "baptism in the Holy Spirit."

Every day was new and exciting as we had a front row seat to God's miracles. In one church a choir girl's short leg grew out three inches in full view of the congregation. Two girls standing next to us fainted! Others cried.

I continued to keep Rose Marie in my prayers. I asked Lori to visit with her again, but she did not want to, and I did not push the issue.

The nation's papers were full of news about the .44 caliber killer in New York City. Someone had been stalking the streets of the Bronx and the borough of Queens killing young women with a .44 caliber Bulldog revolver. In one of his confused notes, the killer referred to himself as "Son of Sam," and the name was picked up by the press. The police had organized a special task force to solve the murders.

Some of the killings took place near my home in Forest Hills, and a double killing took place near the church where I was preaching in the Bronx.

I had assisted the police many times before in various situations, including attempted suicides, and offered to help them now.

I fasted and prayed, asking the Lord's help on the matter. Appeals were put out by the newspapers and the TV and radio stations, stating that a chaplain was on the streets trying to contact "Sam." I walked the deserted streets in Forest Hills between 2:00 and 3:00 A.M. each day, having made prior arrangements with the police to stay clear of my area, hoping the killer would feel free to contact me. I was unarmed and unprotected.

During my prayers, the Holy Spirit had given me a "word of knowledge" about the killer. The information I had given in an interview published in the newspapers and broadcast on television was as follows: "He has a Jewish background and had a deep religious, almost pentecostal, experience at one time. He spends a lot of time in a diner plotting his attacks. Pressure in his head might be caused by a tumor."

At the same time the interview went to press, the police received a note from "Son of Sam," in which there were biblical references, leaving clues as to where he would strike again.

During this time Reverend Stanley Berg called me. Glad Tidings Tabernacle was celebrating its seventieth anniversary on May 7. "Brother Zimmerman will be our speaker," he said. "I know you're a friend of his, and he can use all the support he can get at the moment. Would you be master of ceremonies for the banquet and introduce Brother Zimmerman?"

After the preliminaries of Tom Zimmerman's speech, I rose, gently lifting my hands upward. The audience of several hundred found themselves rising to their feet to give him a standing ovation. Reverend Zimmerman turned his back on the audience to shake my hand and said, "Thanks, Austin."

That night I was again out walking, trying to keep a date with "Son of Sam." The streets were particularly deserted; even the usual number of detective cars were not in the area. The police had reason to believe the killer was preparing to strike in an area of Coney Island and had diverted the task force to this spot.

It was 2:30 A.M. Sunday morning as I walked along a lonely path behind the Forest Hills tennis stadium. I heard a rustle in the bushes nearby—then a sharp metallic click. It had the distinct sound of a gun being cocked. I continued my slow, steady pace. Nothing happened!

Several days later I received a letter from Sally Olsen in Guatemala. She related how on that particular night at 2:30 A.M. she could not sleep and felt an urgent need to pray for me. Also, a woman from Glad Tidings Tabernacle had called my answering service at 2:30 that morning to say she had been awakened from a sound sleep with a strong urge to pray for me.

On Friday, the thirteenth of May, 1977, during an appearance on the national PTL Club television show in Charlotte, North Carolina, I told of my hunt for the killer. I honestly thought that contact with the killer would be made that night, and I asked for everyone's prayers.

When the telecast was over, Lyn McMahan of the production staff came over to me with a worried look. "I don't like the way you said that. Do you feel something is going to happen to you, Austin?" she quizzed me.

"Just pray for me, Lyn," I replied.

After the telecast, Senator Mark Hatfield, who had also been a guest, was with me as we walked through the airport. A woman rushed up to me and said, "I just saw PTL. I will be upholding you in prayer."

I thanked her, said goodbye to Senator Hatfield, and then boarded an Eastern Airlines jet for New York.

That night there was a heavy concentration of detectives around the Forest Hills Inn and train station. Everyone was scared! There were policemen stationed on the roof of the building where I lived. The only area that seemed deserted was in the shadows of the Forest Hills tennis stadium. As I walked near the same spot where I felt the killer had been before, there was a commotion in the bushes.

"Hey," said a voice.

I hesitated, turned around, and stared into a pair of smoldering, glassy eyes.

"I hear you've been looking for me," the face queried.

"That's right, I have," I replied calmly.

"What about–God?" he asked in a squealy, high pitched voice. "Don't you know who I am?" His face contorted to an evil sneer. "I AM THE DEVIL AND I CURSE YOU!"

"IN THE NAME OF JESUS, I RENDER YOU POWERLESS!" I declared emphatically. "YOU CANNOT CURSE ME OR HURT ME!"

"Oh yes I can," he said menacingly. "I will cause your friends and loved ones to turn against you, and I will bring destruction upon your life." Again, the high pitched laugh!

Looking him full in the face, I demanded, "By the blood of Jesus, I command you to get thee behind me Satan!"

A sudden look of terror appeared in his eyes. He turned and disappeared into the shadows. It happened so fast he seemed to have vanished into thin air. The whole encounter probably took no more than two minutes. Had this been the killer, "Son of Sam?"

The following week, the New York Council of the Assemblies of God was to convene in Schenectedy, New York. I made plans to attend as I looked forward to being with my friends.

The first person I met when I arrived was my good friend, Leon Cooke. "Come on," he said warmly, "have lunch with me, Austin." He put his arm around me and said, "You know, you're really a special brother."

I loved Reverend Cooke. We had shared many delightful times together. I had visited his home, shot pool in his basement, and shared with him the challenges of my ministry. We conversed about a multitude of things while we ate together.

"Oh, by the way," he said casually, "a couple of the men would like to talk with you in the side room before the afternoon service."

"That's great," I said, looking forward to more friendly chatter.

We walked into the side room, and I knew immediately that something was wrong. There sat most of the presbytery —staring at me as I walked through the door.

"Sit down," they ordered; then just as abruptly, "Have you been married before?"

Stunned, I replied with a question. "Why do you ask?"

"We received a letter," one of them said.

"What kind of letter? From whom?"

"All right," said my best friend, Reverend Cooke, "it was from Rose Marie. She told me that your real name is not Austin Miles, and . . . ," his voice was somber, "she told me a lot of other things, too."

I realized at that moment that Reverend Cooke had never been told about my first marriage. It was my understanding that Coleman McDuff had cleared the issue with

Springfield headquarters and the New York District before I applied for credentials.

I was sitting in the center of a circle of chairs. Questions began to come at me from all sides.

"Don't you know that a divorced person can't be ordained in the Assemblies of God?"

"Why did you change your name?"

I was bombarded with questions in a relentless attack.

"Can anyone here find any fault with my ministry during the last several years?" I asked, recovering. "Or, in fact, since I started my ministry?"

"No, Brother Miles, your ministry is not in question," they retorted in unison.

"Then this entire meeting is based solely upon the issue of my first marriage?" I was stunned as I looked around the room for support from the ministers I thought were my friends. About half of them had already known about my previous marriage. They all turned their eyes away from me.

"Since I have violated no ministerial or personal ethics, and since this issue goes back fourteen years, I refuse to answer and will ask you to accept my resignation here and now!"

Both Reverend R.D.E. Smith and Stanley Berg spoke up. "No, no, let's not react too quickly. We don't think it will ever come to that, but if it does, we would then let you resign."

They said we could discuss it further at the next *regular* meeting of the presbytery in Syracuse. One by one, they rose to their feet and solemnly left. I sat there alone—shattered—surrounded by a circle of empty chairs.

Oh my God, I anguished, would I be forced out of the church that I loved so much? I put my head in my hands. For the next three hours I sat unmoving, wondering what more could happen in my life.

Outside in the auditorium I could hear hymn singing and preaching. Slowly, I got to my feet and walked quietly to the lobby. I called a taxi and went home to New York City.

I woke up Lori and told her what had happened. I was absolutely heartbroken. She read Scripture to me all night, trying to give me encouragement.

There were more surprises to come. Despite the national publicity about the banking scandal, Reverend Zimmerman was reelected as Superintendent of the Assemblies of God Fellowship at the national convention.

In mid-August the police arrested "Son of Sam," David Berkowitz of Yonkers, and charged him with the murders in the .44 caliber slayings. Berkowitz, a quiet young man, had been raised by a Jewish stepfather. During his youth he had once become a "Jesus freak" and then went on to other things. His own testimony related how, after each killing, he went calmly to the nearest diner and sat it out while the excitement raged all around. After he was sentenced for the murders, they took him to prison, and preparation was made to do a brain scan.

I stared at the newspaper transfixed by the face of David Berkowitz. It was the face that had spoken to me from the bushes. I stared in horror, remembering the wild eyes and the sinister laugh. Most of all, I remembered the "curse." Little did I know that the greatest "spiritual battle" of my life lay just ahead!

# 29
# The Vision

Notification came from Syracuse, New York, that I was expected to come to a presbyters' meeting in July. I told them that I had church services booked during July's meeting and felt my first obligation was to keep my dates with the pastors who had advertised these services. They agreed in writing to delay my hearing until January 17, 1978, at 2:00 P.M.

Nevertheless, I began to get frantic telephone calls from pastors with whom I had services booked in advance. . . . Cancellations came in droves. Angry, confused, and downright hostile, I called Reverend R.D.E. Smith at his home in Binghamton, New York, and told him what had been happening. "Brother Smith," I said, "I've had it. I'm sending in my resignation."

"I'm sorry, you can't do that," he informed me. "Once a charge has been placed against you and a meeting of the presbytery is scheduled, you cannot resign. You must abide by their verdict."

One of the places where I had not been cancelled was in Millville, New Jersey, where I had been scheduled for a full week of services in May. The public bus I had to take in order to get there rumbled and rattled along as I watched quaint little towns, then open fields, flash by the window. I tried to determine to what extent God would use me.

"Is the bus station located in the center of Millville?" I asked the driver.

"Ain't no bus station there," said the driver. "We let the Millville passengers out at Wa Wa's."

"Wa Wa what??" I asked.

"Wa Wa's," said the driver. "It's a store."

An old model car was parked nearby, and two men got out as the bus stopped. Pastor Gerritt Kenyon came on board the bus to welcome me even before I had a chance to grab my bag and get off. Outside stood a broad, husky man who looked like a lumberjack. "This is Luther McDonald, our song leader," the pastor explained, introducing us.

"Praise the Lord!" Luther exclaimed exuberantly, and before I knew what was happening, he had embraced me in a giant bear hug that lifted me off my feet. I thoroughly expected to hear my ribs pop. This boisterous welcome lifted my spirits as well as my body. It was so good to see a friendly face.

The church had an evangelist's quarters in the main building where the sanctuary was located. This was to be my home for the next week.

There was a spirit of peace in the big, comfortable church with its relaxing color schemes and its sanctuary gently illuminated by a big cross at the back of the platform. I enjoyed the moments during the wee hours, having the church all to myself.

Desperately I cried out to God in my loneliness. "Lord, I can endure anything as long as I know that Your anointing is upon me and this ministry will further the Gospel. Please deliver me from anger and unforgiveness and keep me in peace upon Your path, with joy in my heart."

Sunday morning is when the evangelist is expected to make his best impression. It is also the time when all official announcements are made. Usually, I sat like a robot on the platform through these preliminaries. The secret of success in the Sunday morning service is not how well you preach, but how well you sit, stand, sit, stand, sit again, and "amen" the pastor. I had said over and over to myself I would only preach the evening services.

Yet, there I was, Sunday morning, May 29, 1977, at the First Assembly of God Church on Wheaton Avenue in Millville. The moment I walked onto the platform with Pastor Kenyon, I felt a pulling to turn my head to a section of the front row. I found myself eye to eye with a slim, attractive woman with short cut hair. Her mouth seemed ready to drop open as sheer astonishment was manifested in her face.

"Good Lord," I thought, "What have I done wrong now?" Had I already met with a member's disapproval? Maybe it was something else. I subtly glanced down. My socks matched. Then a sense of horror flooded me. I was glad when the pastor asked everyone to bow their heads in prayer. I quickly checked to see if perhaps I had failed to activate my zipper. Negative—to my relief. After prayer, I glanced again at her. The expression was the same.

She was sitting with two beautiful blonde girls, obviously her daughters. Although a bit on the frail side, one was delicately lovely, and when she worshipped, I found myself glancing down at her. Lifting her hands to God, she was what I would have imagined an angel to look like.

Following the service I had Sunday dinner with the pastor and his wife.

"How's the evangelist's quarters?" Pastor Kenyon asked.

"Oh, fine," I said. My rooms had special appeal to me because of their location right off the sanctuary where I had planned for a lot of prayer that week.

"You'll have a TV tomorrow," Reverend Kenyon said. "There are some people who come to the church who own a furniture store, and they are having a TV set brought in for your use during your stay."

How very considerate, I thought, people who really have a concern for the personal needs of a visiting evangelist.

The Sunday night service brought a fine response, and more than expected were there for Memorial Day. Shortly after I began, I glanced down at the front row to my right. The woman with her two daughters was in the same place, only now there seemed to be more family members with her. The woman still had that puzzled expression on her face. She seemed to be studying me with unusual scrutiny. I was certain we had never met. At one point during the sermon on faith, I glanced down at the daughters. The frail one seemed lifted to another plane in her abandoned worship. There was such a sweetness about her that in spite of myself I thought, "Now there is exactly the kind of girl I would like to have married." I quickly dismissed the thought, as the entire idea was too preposterous to consider.

After the service the pastor requested my attendance at a party for the church young people to be held in his basement recreation room. I really was not in the mood to socialize, so I sat quietly in the farthest corner I could find, sipping punch and nibbling cake.

A great deal of excitement was taking place near me. An extremely handsome young man was in an all-out, fight to the finish, table tennis match with one of the blonde girls from the front pew. I learned her name was Holly and his name was Sam. Holly, a pretty, athletic girl, had kicked off her shoes and was in serious competition with Sam, a champion wrestling coach, who was known to excel in any sport he tackled. Now in full view of his peer group, Samuel Siligato had met his match. With a final swat of the paddle, a wild cheer erupted from the kids in the basement. Holly had won! After the contest, as the two laughed and talked, it appeared that Cupid had swapped his bow and arrow for a ping pong paddle and had already put the net around them.

At that moment, several blocks from the church, Grace Davis, the mother of the two blondes, was nervously pacing back and forth in her bedroom. "I don't understand it," she was saying to herself. "He must be married because he mentioned his daughter in the sermon this morning."

The Davis family, although not members of the church, were friends of the pastor and came from time to time. Two weeks before I had come, Pastor Kenyon had handed out some pamphlets announcing my services and had asked members of the congregation to "spread the word."

Sitting in her office in the furniture store, ready to stuff the flyer announcing my services into an envelope, Grace Davis felt a gentle vibration go through her body, then a "picture" manifested before her eyes. Grace did not know how to cope with this. She stared more intently at my photo. The words came clearly. "Austin Miles and Valerie . . . travel . . . then marriage."

"Dear heavens," Grace thought, "I've flipped my lid. I've never even met this man."

For ten days she conveniently pushed the words out of her mind, until that Sunday morning. The moment I walked out onto the platform, the "picture" hit her again—this time with more impact than ever. "Austin Miles and Valerie . . . travel . . . then marriage." The words were bright and clear as they vividly dominated her mind. That was the reason she had been looking at me so strangely.

Following the Sunday night service, Grace went directly home to sleep. At 5:30 A.M. Monday morning, she was rudely awakened by another bright "picture" that illuminated the bedroom. "Austin and Valerie . . . travel . . . then marriage." She was perplexed. She still had not met me.

On Tuesday morning at 5:30 A.M. it happened again; only this time something else happened after the "picture." A loud voice out of the ceiling ordered, "Tell it to someone!"

Grace, by now, was up and pacing the room more nervously than ever. "No!" she argued with the voice in the ceiling. "You must be crazy! Seeing a picture is one thing, telling someone is ridiculous."

"Tell someone!" the voice commanded, as she felt a strong push on her back from an unseen force.

Crying, not knowing how to deal with this new intrusion in her life, Grace went to her furniture store. The first person she saw was her trusted friend who had worked for the family for years. Her name was Sylvia Bogan. "Sylvia," Grace said hesitantly, "please do me a favor. Take a piece of paper, write down what I have to tell you, then put it someplace where nobody will ever find it. Don't tell anybody, unless it comes to pass."

Sylvia Bogan found it difficult to keep her face calm as Grace gave her the message. "Austin Miles and Valerie . . . travel . . . then marriage."

"Poor Mrs. Davis," Sylvia thought sadly, as she dutifully complied with her employer's request.

Still being compelled by the push against her back, Grace left the store to give the message as directed to another friend, Shirley Sheppard. Shirley wrote the message on her calendar, and then the invisible hand pushing against Grace's back disappeared.

The services Tuesday were being especially blessed with Divine healings. I looked with anticipation at the front row where the attractive family sat together. They all held hands during prayer. Sam was now sitting next to Holly with the family. It appeared that his defeat in ping pong had brought him a great victory—a lovely girlfriend and a new family.

How I longed for such a family. I had no brothers or sisters, and now with my marriage ended, it looked as though I would only be able to enjoy such a family life vicariously from a distance. I glanced down again at the frail little blonde with her hands lifted toward heaven. It gave me pleasure just to look at her.

"Who is that family that always sits in the front row?" I asked.

"That's the Davis family," Reverend Kenyon answered, munching a piece of toast. "They own the furniture store," he added.

"Is that all one family?" I asked.

He nodded affirmatively.

"What are their names?"

"Bob and Grace," he said.

"And the two blonde girls, are they the daughters?"

"Yes," he replied, "the youngest one is Holly, and the oldest one is Valerie."

Usually I vanished after the service to get away by myself as quickly as possible. This night, however, I went among the people and stopped to say hello to the Davis family as they were leaving. "It is so wonderful to see a family as close as yours seems to be," I said to the mother. "It's really refreshing."

Following the service, I once again enjoyed the private time of fellowship with Reverend Kenyon before going into the sanctuary to pray. He had been a gracious host whose deep commitment to God's work touched my heart. When he informed me about an event that was taking place, it made me realize the great responsibility I had in handling the vessels of God.

"The Davis family has arranged for an ambulance plane to bring Bob's mother here from Florida," he revealed. "She has been very ill. They want the grandmother to have the benefit of your prayers. They're sending over a special lounge chair for her to lie on during tomorrow night's service. It will be down front near the altar."

Retiring to the evangelist's quarters, I tried to sleep. Bringing God's word forth was such an awesome responsibility. Dressed in bathrobe and pajamas, I returned to the altar.

The next morning, after only a couple hours of sleep, I was again at the altar. I noticed the lounge chair had already been brought in and placed down front. It was then God spoke to me and directed me to fast for the service that night. "You yield your body to Me in total obedience, and that healing will take place, rewarding those who have placed such faith in your prayers."

I went to the Kenyons and shared with them God's command to me. I drank three cups of hot water and spent the rest of the day in prayer.

A large crowd greeted me Thursday night. Instead of my usual light-hearted remarks, I opened with a solemn prayer.

The Holy Spirit had begun working already, and the message seemed to have a special anointing. I could feel anticipation building up as the presence of Jesus became very real.

After the message, prayers for healing began, and throughout the auditorium people seemed to be receiving a touch from God. I left the platform to walk down to the woman on the lounge chair, anointing her with oil. There was a tremendous flow going through my fingers. I had obeyed God's commands, and there was no hesitation for me to say, "In the name of Jesus Christ of Nazareth rise up and walk!"

I reached out to her. She took my hands and slowly got off the lounge and began to walk with me. Rejoicing broke out all over the auditorium. Members of the Davis family knelt at the altar, thanking God. The woman looked toward them with tears in her eyes. "That means more to me than anything," she said, "to see my son kneeling at the altar."

As people came forward to the altar to pray, I walked to the rear of the platform, and with my back toward everyone knelt beneath the huge cross, asking God to meet all the needs represented there. All at once great excitement broke out at the altar as both Holly and Valerie received the "baptism in the Holy Spirit."

It was very late by the time the service ended and the church was cleared. God had been faithful and powerful. It was a victorious week, and I was reminded once again that if we obey God in all that He requires of us, NOTHING IS IMPOSSIBLE.

On Friday, the closing night of the service, there was a long prayer line. The presence of the Holy Spirit was so strong that many people could not stand under His power. I asked everyone who had received from God during the week to thank Jesus for what He had done, emphasizing that only Jesus heals.

There were only a few hours left for rest before rising at 5 A.M. I had no idea of the extent of the tremendous miracle that had occurred and would soon be confirmed.

Reverend Kenyon drove me to the Philadelphia airport, where I flew out to Milwaukee for a new series of meetings.

As the plane roared down the runway and into the air, I settled back, peaceful in spirit and happy in heart for the first time in a long while. I hadn't the slightest idea that the best was yet to come as God's hand was molding a new life for me.

# 30
# Valerie's Story

During my week in Millville, Valerie Davis was having an encounter with the Lord which would profoundly affect my future. Here is the account taken directly from her journal.

*On Sunday morning, May 29, 1977, our family walked into the Millville Assembly of God Church. We were very new Christians. My sister Holly and I were almost defiant. An evangelist, Austin Miles, was the guest speaker for the week-long revival services.*

*We had been very open to God until the previous evening. On the spur of the moment we had decided to visit another church in another town where a married couple were preaching. What we encountered turned us off so completely we were now questioning the entire Christian religion.*

*At this meeting the evangelists were having a prayer line. Holly and I went forward. The woman told me to close my eyes. When I did, she lightly pressed on the side of my neck, and as I started to lose consciousness, she gently pushed on my stomach. The next thing I remembered, I was lying on the floor surrounded by people saying, "Praise the Lord, she has been slain in the Spirit!"*

*Tremendously confused and desperately needing help, I wanted to feel close to God for strength and reassurance. I started saying, "Thank you, Jesus," over and over again quietly with my eyes closed. Several people nearby shouted, "No! Don't say that! Don't speak in English, you're fighting the Holy Spirit!"*

*Embarrassed, I thought, "What is wrong with a Christian saying, 'Thank you, Jesus'?" How had I gotten myself into this predicament? Holly was on the floor next to me. Looking over at her, I wondered what she was feeling. Then to my relief, my mother came and knelt down beside me and said, "Come on, Valerie; it's all right."*

*Several women harshly told her, "You shouldn't touch anyone while they're in the Spirit." She ignored them and patted my head, smiling reassuringly. Anger suddenly filled me. I wasn't "in the Spirit," whatever that was. I was simply lying on the floor too ashamed to get up. I was mad at myself, mostly, for letting myself be played for a fool.*

*Mother helped me to my feet, then rescued Holly, who was having exactly the same experience. Then she went up and stood in front of the woman evangelist. Quietly we went and stood next to her. The woman asked my mother, "Do you want the Holy Spirit?"*

*My mother looked her directly in the eyes and answered, "I am open for any gift GOD chooses to give me. I never ask God for gifts. Whatever He wants me to have I will accept."*

*The woman then told Mom to close her eyes. My mother stood still. I could feel the tension in the air as everyone watched. The woman pressed so hard on her neck and stomach I thought she would hurt her. My mother had about her an aura of quiet confidence and determination. Suddenly, I knew that the lady evangelist would NEVER be able to push my mother down. After what seemed an emotional eternity, my mother opened her eyes and looked directly at the minister.*

*Shocked, the woman jumped back about three feet, exclaiming, "Everyone* I *touch falls down. There must be something you haven't renounced that is keeping you from the Holy Spirit!"*

*My mother, with a loving smile, reached forward, and gently held her and said, "I am very sorry I disappointed* you. *It just was not meant to be."*

*I could feel the hatred from the woman and the confusion from everyone around us. We turned and walked out of the church.*

*The next morning Holly and I had decided we did not want to go to the Millville church. Mother calmly told us we were to get dressed and to come downstairs. Then she would tell us exactly what had happened to us the preceding evening.*

*She explained that a hypnotic trick had been used on us. Mother then used the same pressure technique on Holly, and she wound up on the floor. She then told us we shouldn't judge all Christians because we had one bad experience. She asked us to at least give Reverend Austin Miles a chance.*

*So, we reluctantly agreed to go to church. At this time we did not know that Mom had received her "picture."*

*As Reverend Austin Miles started to speak, electricity filled the air. I was completely caught up with his enthusiasm and love of Jesus. I shivered with goose bumps as he gave his testimony.*

*At the end of the first service he asked all of us to go into prayer as he started to call out illnesses and took authority over each one in the name of Jesus. Afterwards, I sat quietly, my thoughts racing. I had been sick for twenty-seven years. I desperately wanted to believe I could be healed.*

*I went every night with my mother and Holly, becoming more expectant over the possibility that I would receive the "baptism in the Holy Spirit" and the healing I needed.*

*On Wednesday Mom had a "picture" of my Dad's mother in Florida. We had not heard from her in six months. She saw Grandmom, lying in bed in a pink floral nightgown, very ill. Mother called and arranged for a plane to fly her in with ambulance service.*

*On Thursday we put Grandmom in a lounge chair in front of our first row pew. Our entire family, Mom, Dad, Holly, I, and my brother Gary, were there.*

*Reverend Miles had everyone hold hands as he preached a sermon, "Love Motivating the Holy Spirit." He came down and anointed Grandmom with oil. After prayer, she felt enough strength to get up and walk around. Our entire family, so grateful, knelt at the altar to thank Jesus for the healing touch our grandmother had received. It was the first time my father had ever gone to the altar. Holly and I were so happy that Dad had finally been moved enough to do this we started saying quietly, "Thank you, Jesus, for Daddy . . . ," over and over.*

*Suddenly, we were both aware of a tugging sensation coming from the cross in front of the altar. I looked up and saw Reverend Miles on his knees praying under the cross. Before we knew what hit us, first Holly started shaking violently, then my throat became paralyzed, and I couldn't speak a word of English. The only sounds that came out were strange, unknown words. Holly and I grabbed hands and laughed and cried at the same time when we realized we were being baptized in the Holy Spirit. We were filled with overflowing love, peace, and joy.*

*On Friday night we both stood before the service began and gave our testimonies.*

*After the service I stood in the prayer line, suffering from a terrible headache and a fever of 101°. Reverend Miles looked at me with compassion and asked what was wrong. I answered, "I have been sick most of my life."*

*He lightly anointed my forehead with oil. As he was praying for me, all the stress came out of my body, starting from my toes and going through the top of my head. He excitedly said, "Here it comes, sister!"*

*I floated gently backwards to the floor. My fever broke. My headache was gone! "Mommy," I said delightedly, after I rose from the floor, "I am healed!"*

*I arrived home around 11:30 P.M. on Friday, June 3. Whew! What a week it had been. For the first time in my life I knew what a healing and revival ministry was.*

*I chatted joyfully with Holly and Mom for a few minutes, then went to bed exhausted and fell into a sound sleep. It was 12:30 A.M., June 4.*

*Fifteen minutes later I awoke with a violent headache. I was in shock; I could not understand it. Grabbing my Bible, I remembered some passages. "No! I don't believe this! I claimed my healing!" Then I stated even more firmly, "I stand on your Word, God." The headache still stayed. I was distraught and confused.*

*The headache persisted for an hour. Tears started streaming down my face. I finally said, "O.K., Lord, if this headache is not a trick from Satan–if it is truly from You–* tell me why!"

*At this time I was lying on my back trying to lift my hands up to the Lord. I was still clutching the Bible tightly. Suddenly, as I said the words "tell me why" a strange power overcame me. I breathed so slowly that soon I wasn't breathing at all. Somewhat unconscious, I suddenly realized my heart wasn't beating either! A sense of fear struck me and through my strange semi-consciousness, I pulled my right hand over to take the pulse on my left wrist. There wasn't any! As my fear became panic, my pulse started beating again.*

*In an instant I became earthly conscious again. It was then that my violent headache returned. A very strong command said,* "Again." *I clutched my Bible even tighter, saying, "God, You know I don't know many Scriptures by heart, so all I can do is say I stand on Your Word and if this is Your will, go ahead." I was terrified.*

*Immediately the same power took over. It was like being in an unexplainable suspended animation. The first thing I saw was myself lying in a coffin in front of the altar at our church. I was dead. I felt this strong tugging sensation pulling me toward the coffin.*

*My tears started flowing again. Instantly God gently but firmly rebuked me. I said, "I'm not crying for me God, but for my family. You know how much we all love each other. I just testified earlier that I was healed. What will they think? How will they take my death?"*

*There was silence—God did not answer.*

*I went on with the questions I wanted most to be answered before I died. I lifted all the names of my family to Him and asked if they had accepted Jesus. He answered yes to them. I then lifted names of other relatives and close friends. God said yes to a few, others were "very close," and sometimes, "Their lives are still in their own hands."*

*After asking these questions, I told God, "O.K., Lord, only You know how everyone will accept this, so I put my life in Your hands." The coffin vanished. I was baffled.*

*As I was trying to overcome my surprise at this return of my life, the coffin dramatically reappeared! I questioned God, "Why, after all these twenty-seven years of my being so sick, did You bother to heal me if You intended to take my life the same night?"*

*Then God answered every important question I ever had. He said I had wanted to die for a long time. I knew this was certainly true. I couldn't accept a life of hospitalizations and the feelings of hopelessness that come from having an illness that can't be helped. I always felt I was a burden on my family, even though they showered me with love.*

*God said, "You prayed for death—I am now answering that prayer."*

*I pleaded, "God, I only wanted to die because my illness made life so meaningless. Now that I am healed I don't feel that way at all! For the first time I have a strong reason to want to live. But, if it is Your will to take my life, I give it to You; it is Yours."*

*At once the vivid coffin went away! Now I was thoroughly confused. What next???*

*Then I began to feel a very warm pressure flowing over my stomach and both sides.*

*"Oh! Is He going to burn me to death?" I wondered, terrified.*

*"No," God assured me. The voice seemed amused. "You are being healed! Just like Austin Miles said he'd been healed!"*

*I was so overcome with joy that I started laughing and crying at the same time.*

*The burning pressure moved to my heart. It felt as if God's Hand was massaging and rebuilding my heart. I thought, "He has my heart and my life in His Hand." The healing flow stayed at my heart for so long I finally asked, "Why are You spending so much time on my heart?"*

*God answered strongly, "You had a very weak heart. All the years of stress, illness, and fevers have taken their toll." Then in writing flashed the words RHEUMATIC FEVER. I was shocked!*

*God continued to heal me all night. Warmth and tingling flooded the front side of my body.*

*"Turn over on your stomach," I was told. Still clutching my Bible, I felt God's warm tingling healing flow throughout the back side of my body from head to toe.*

*Just as I thought the healing was finished, He solemnly said, "Now curl into a fetal position. You were sick since birth, even while you were in the womb. I am going to give you a PHYSICAL REBIRTH." Curling into this position, the flow went through me, completing the healing. He said I was taken back to birth to remove all the physical and emotional scars, which were very deep.*

*Then I was given more explanations and commands.*

*God said, "You have learned deep compassion for others through your many years of illness and hospitalizations. I know twenty-seven years seems like a long time to you, but time is unimportant to ME as you know it.* I *will fill the void in your life. YOU are going to be used in a healing ministry.* I *have a very definite plan. You will know exactly what to do with your life in just* one month!"

*I panicked at the idea of being used in a healing ministry. I had always been terribly shy.*

*"I'm not ready for something like this, God!" I pleaded. "How about if I go to Bible school for eight or ten years?" That would have given me plenty of time to get used to the whole idea.*

*"No!" came the firm reply as He interrupted my thoughts. "You are not to go to Bible school. Man may teach you wrong. Just read My Word, the Bible. Commit it to memory.* I *will teach you . . . and Austin Miles will teach you."*

*The latter part of this statement flabbergasted me. "Austin Miles?" I protested. "Why I don't even know him!"*

*To my shock, He replied, "You will! You are going to fill a void in Austin Miles' life. He is very lonely due to the heartbreak of a broken marriage."*

*My shock turned to embarrassment as God revealed this personal aspect of Reverend Miles' life.*

*"Am I going to marry him?" It seemed the only logical answer to filling the void he was talking about.*

*"Don't worry," He said reassuringly, "I will never ask you to carry any burden you are unable to bear."*

*God told me to tell my mother and sister everything that had transpired between us so they would understand. Then Mrs. Anita Kenyon, the local pastor's wife, would have to be told to write it down, and then after these people were informed, I was to tell Austin Miles.*

*It was 6 A.M., and the dawn was just beginning to filter into my bedroom when I arose from my bed and entered my sister's bedroom. There was a strange sensation of energy emanating from me, a sort of oily electrical flow.*

*Puff, our cat, was sleeping at the foot of Holly's bed. He had been very sick and had a large weeping cyst on his abdomen. Automatically, as if he knew what I was going to do, Puff turned over and exposed his sore stomach to me. I put my hands directly over the area and began praying, "A prayer of faith shall save the sick and the Lord shall raise him up" (James 5:15). All of a sudden, an indelible impression in vivid color showed me the horrible, ugly abscess inside Puff's stomach. Next, a tremendous burst of energy darted from my hands into the cat. The infection disappeared!*

*Puff jumped up and began to purr and prance around on the bed just as Holly woke up. We both cried as I told her everything that had happened; then we rushed in to tell Mom.*

*"Let me see that cat!" she exclaimed as she turned Puff over to examine his stomach. The cyst was gone, and his entire belly was covered with new pink skin!*

*Later in the afternoon I gave Mrs. Kenyon my testimony as God had commanded, and she wrote it all down. I cried a lot just reliving it. Once, when I tried to bring up the part about Austin and the personal aspect of his life, she snapped back with, "I am sure his wife is under great conviction!" She then looked at me with such a questioning glare that I was intimidated. As a minister's wife she wouldn't understand. Small wonder! It had happened to me, and I had difficulty understanding it!*

# 31

# One Month to the Day

In the Wisconsin church each night before services started, I found myself glancing down front at the empty pew and thinking of the Davis family. Oh, how I wished they were here. Particularly Valerie. I remembered her angelic, serene face as she stood with the congregation, tears of joy rolling down her face as she praised God with uplifted hands.

After returning from the trip, I thumbed through my usual thick stack of accumulated mail. My heart skipped a beat and with a great anticipation I tore open the letter. The return address on the envelope said "Davis Furniture." Above it was the name Valerie Davis.

I eagerly savored every word as she related that she had received a Divine healing that was very unusual. When Val had asked Mrs. Kenyon to write to me about her healing, Mrs. Kenyon surprisingly told Valerie to write to me herself.

Valerie suggested that I bring my family with me when I preached in Bridgeton, New Jersey. There we might get together for a chat.

Bridgeton, New Jersey? Where was that? I checked my calendar. The Bridgeton services were scheduled in another week. I checked a road map. Bridgeton was only twelve miles from Millville.

I never booked crusades in locations close to a church I had just served. It must have been booked during a period of time when requests were coming in so fast and furious I didn't have a chance to check the locations.

I felt anticipation rise within me at the thought of seeing Valerie again. I wrote to her and told her I would be at the church over the Fourth of July.

The entire Davis family was seated in the front row of the Bridgeton church. Sammy was also there, with Holly. After service that morning, I had hoped to see Valerie, but the entire family left immediately after the meeting.

That afternoon I telephoned her and asked her to meet me in the pastor's home after the evening service. She agreed. Then I asked if she were free the next day, the Fourth of July.

"Yes," she replied.

"Good," I said. "You can tell me about your healing. Is it all right with you if we spend a quiet day on the beach and just talk?" I asked, looking forward to getting away from the crowds.

Then, other words came out that I had not planned. "Promise me one thing," I said. "During our talk tomorrow tell me whatever is on your heart, and I will do the same. Can it be a no holds barred conversation?"

"That's agreed," she said.

It was a sunny, warm Fourth of July, a perfect day for a beach outing. Valerie picked me up in a family car, and we drove toward Cape May. This would be the first time we would be alone together. It was extremely comfortable for both of us. "I was so glad to get your letter," I began, as we drove.

"Were you really?" she asked, smiling.

"Yes," I said, "but you really did not have to put in the letter that you were the blonde girl with the sister and family, etc., etc., etc. I knew right away who you were."

"First of all," she said, "I hesitated to write you. I didn't want you to think I was crazy or forward. I would not have written if Mrs. Kenyon hadn't suggested it. I really didn't think you would remember who I was, since you meet so many people."

I started to say something about how I had thought of her every night, picturing her in every front row of every service I had preached. I stopped myself before starting.

"You were going to say something," she said.

"No, never mind," I replied. For some reason I realized once again that I was just plain shy on a one to one basis, especially with girls.

"Didn't we agree at your suggestion that this would be a 'no holds barred' conversation?" she prompted.

"Yes, we did," I said, grateful that she had helped me over a rough spot in our talk. "O.K. I wanted more than anything to get in contact with you after I left Millville, only I didn't know how. When your letter came, I frankly jumped for joy."

We rode silently for awhile. "There is something I must say to you," Valerie began. "I don't quite know how to tell you or how you will react to it."

"Remember our agreement. Just say whatever is on your mind."

She sighed, groping for the right words. "I was sick for twenty-seven years with severe allergies. I was in and out of hospitals all my life. God healed me in your services, and I've been fine ever since. I have more energy than I have ever had in my life. I feel marvelous."

"That's wonderful," I exclaimed. "Praise God."

"There's more," she said. "When I got home after church that evening, the healing lasted all night. God spoke to me audibly during that time. He . . . mentioned . . . you."

Gathering up courage, she continued. "God said to me, 'You are going to fill a void in Austin's life.' I don't completely understand, but it seemed to mean that my life—and your life—were to somehow be together." She was obviously nervous about telling me this and quickly added, "Please don't think I'm silly, but God told me to tell you everything. That you would know the significance of it all."

"The significance is probably far more than you realize," I said, "and even I am a little boggled at the moment. Honestly, Valerie . . . I have thought of little else than you from the first time I saw you."

We rode in silence for several miles. My right hand gently released from the steering wheel and eased down to the seat where her hand was resting.

We got out of the car on Cape May beach and began to walk, hand in hand, near the water. Suddenly I stopped. She looked up at me. "Valerie," I blurted out, "I believe God has sent you to me. Will you marry me?" My own words which seemed to pop out on their own jolted me when I realized what I had said.

"Yes," she answered calmly.

There, on the beach, we made vows before God that since He had put us together, we would recognize that this was more than a commitment of two people, but a spiritual union ordained by God Himself to last forever.

Near us on the beach was some sort of rock formation that appeared to be a half-built igloo-type house. "Look," I said, "we've already been given an official house." I picked her up and carried her over the imaginary threshhold and through the opening. "Not bad," I observed. "A few repairs, and it will be as good as new."

We laughed, played in the sand, and ran barefoot on the warm beach. That night we had dinner in a big seafood restaurant located on a pier. After dinner we sat on the end of the pier and talked while the Fourth of July fireworks lit up the sky in the distance.

Valerie ran through the front door of her house. "Mother," she yelled, "Where are you?"

"Up here," Grace answered from her bedroom. She and Holly were in the room waiting for Valerie's return. Grace had finally told Holly the episode surrounding her strange "picture."

"Mom, you'll never guess what happened," Valerie said, sitting at the foot of her mother's bed.

"Try me," her mother said, smiling knowingly.

"Austin Miles proposed to me!" she exclaimed. "And I accepted."

Her mother took her hand gently as she recounted the entire "picture" phenomenon, whom she had told, and why she had not told Valerie.

"What?" exclaimed Val in surprise. "You kept this a secret from me for over a month?" She quickly looked at the calendar. It was July 4! It was *June* 4 when God spoke to Valerie telling her that she would know what she would do with her life exactly one month later. It was exactly *one month to the day!*

# 32
# Engaged

"I'll drive you back to New York," Valerie said to me the day after my final church service in Bridgeton.

"Oh, no, it's too long a trip for you to make and then return alone," I said. "Just drop me where I can catch the bus."

I wanted to stop by Pastor Kenyon's to say hello. The Kenyons responded uneasily to the fact that Valerie had brought me there. As we drove away from their house, Valerie said, "I insist on driving you home. It will give us more time to talk and will give me a chance to meet your daughter."

We continued to argue on the way to the bus station. I didn't want her to have to make the four hour drive, but Lori was due back from a summer Bible camp, and the timing seemed right. We finally agreed and drove past the station and on to New York.

The minute we arrived at my New York apartment, there was an emergency phone call. A fourteen-year-old girl named Ruth Sebastiano had just broken her neck in a swimming pool accident. The family had been trying to reach me from the moment it happened. Ruth had been taken to a hospital in Hartford, Connecticut.

Valerie smiled as I asked for directions to the hospital. She had been praying that I would go. Since I did not have a car, it would have been impossible for me to get to Hartford if Val had not been there. We left immediately.

I had first met Ruth Ann Sebastiano while holding healing services in Waterbury, Connecticut. She was a beautiful, deaf fourteen-year-old, with black curly hair. After the service Ruth Ann came to me and asked for prayer that she might be able to hear her mother's voice just once. God granted Ruth's request after our prayer together. This led her to a special ministry for the "deaf" even though her healing was not permanent.

As I entered the intensive care room, it was obvious that Ruthie was in severe pain. She was stretched out in traction and had been given less than a thirty percent chance to live.

The Hartford Hospital report, case number 154-58-15, signed by Dr. N. Gahm dated 7-4-77 stated: "*Final* diagnosis: Fracture–dislocation of cervical spine quadriplegia." In the report it described the accident, ". . . She immediately experienced a loss of sensation below the neck as well as the inability to move her arms and her legs."

When I looked at Ruthie she said, "Praise God . . . Jesus is going to use this for His glory!!!"

"Ruthie," I assured her, "God is going to intervene. You are His servant and He is not going to let this be permanent. Not only are you going to walk again, but we are going to ask Jesus that the pressure from that dive will cause your hearing to be restored and that this entire incident will be used for God's glory." I held her hand tenderly as I spoke the following words. "Ruthie, some day soon *you will walk through the doors of the PTL Club and tell the entire world how God performed a miracle through all this.*"

After anointing her with oil, her mother and I took authority over the illness, using Mark 16:18, ". . . They shall lay hands on the sick, and they shall recover."

Her mother began to touch various parts of her body, and Ruthie said she could feel her mother's touch. There was no doubt in my mind that Ruthie would recover as the Holy Spirit ministered so beautifully in that hospital room.

By the time we arrived back in New York City, I had missed the evening train to upstate New York, where I was booked for a Full Gospel Businessmen's breakfast. There was no train the following morning that would get me there on time, so Valerie stayed in New York so she could drive me to the meeting.

At this prayer meeting we both put our petitions before the Lord. "Jesus, we want our union to be pleasing in Your sight. If this is not pleasing to You, then we will know by the results of the following service."

This was a new chapter of the Full Gospel Businessmen's Fellowship International. Valerie supported me in prayer as I prayed for the sick while receiving the "word of knowledge." The results were remarkable. Eighty percent of the people stood and confirmed healings. There seemed to be a greater freedom of the Holy Spirit's flow through me than I had felt any time during my ministry. We thanked God as we understood this to be His sanction of our union.

Val and Lori hit it off beautifully. I had another long trip ahead for a week of services. "Dad," Lori asked, "while you're gone this time, could I go home with Valerie?" Lori had prayed to get away from the city and all the sad memories. Her prayers were answered.

I was spending as much time as possible visiting Valerie and Lori at the Davis home between the few speaking engagements I had left by now! Rumors were rampant! Still, there had been no official charges filed by the presbytery.

I was happy to look at my schedule and see that I was still booked in Minot, North Dakota, with Reverend Richard Orchard. In my opinion he was the greatest Bible teacher and scholar I had ever met. He was also a concert accordianist with an explosive sense of humor, in addition to being a man of steady prayer. Many times late at night I found him in the sanctuary praying for God's supreme guidance. I had grown to respect and love Brother Orchard.

When I visited his beautiful church in Minot, I shared with him the problems facing my ministry.

"Don't feel too badly about all this," Reverend Orchard said to me jovially as we walked across an open field. "The way things are, I don't think there's one character in the Bible who would be accepted for preaching in our church today."

Taking a deep breath of pure North Dakota air, Richard Orchard continued with his observation. "Stop and think about it. David committed murder so he could commit adultery. Abraham lied about his wife in Egypt. The district could never grant him credentials. Jacob was a conniver, a real con man. The church would never accept him."

"On the contrary," I interrupted with mock seriousness, "that might qualify him to be a superintendent."

"You might be right at that," Brother Orchard acquiesced laughingly. "Then there was Solomon with a thousand wives, concubines, and mistresses. This out-and-out swinger would never be tolerated. James and John were so violent that they were called 'brothers of thunder.' They certainly did not exhibit a meek, peaceful spirit. Paul and Barnabas got into such a scrap that they cancelled an entire missionary tour, and Jesus Himself was called a wine-bibber and a glutton. He never got along with the church hierarchy, so he would *automatically* be out."

I found myself joining in with the absurdity of the whole situation.

"Sure," I said, "after Noah built his ark, he went out and got drunk. Once that got back to the church, he would have been kicked out." We both sat down on a bank. I picked a shaft of straw and chewed on the end of it. "You know," I said, "the only possible biblical character that might be accepted in the church was Daniel, but then again he could never hold an office because he didn't speak in tongues."

As we both had a good laugh over that one, Brother Orchard added a final observation. "You know, the lions in that cage were smarter than our church officers. Those lions knew Daniel was a good preacher and left him alone. But the church hierarchy gobbles up good preachers every day."

The week with Brother Orchard was a tonic I very much needed. Once again God put the right man in my path at exactly the right time.

The services were going well, and the attendance continued to build as the Lord performed miracles. It was difficult to say goodbye to Reverend Richard Orchard at the conclusion of the week.

I had already rearranged most of my schedule due to the many cancellations when Simon Vikse, an international director of the Full Gospel Businessmen, on the spur of the moment suggested having me go with him on an airlift to Europe. Impulsively, I said yes.

I went directly from North Dakota to New York to pack before joining the group at Kennedy Airport for the trip. Then, Simon Vikse, Clinton Utterback, an extremely talented pianist-singer, and I boarded Air India for London.

When we arrived in London, we were informed that we were to speak that same night. As overtired with jet lag as I was, there was still such an anointing on the service that all of us were refreshed. The next day Clinton accompanied me on a visit to the main shopping area of London. I knew Valerie's birthday was coming up, and I wanted to get her an engagement ring. I had very little money, but we found exactly the one I wanted, delicate enough for her small hand. We arrived back at the church just in time for our evening service.

From London we went to Paris and from there to Norway. We arrived in Bergen just in time to be taken from the airplane directly to the State Lutheran Church for the services.

Working with an interpreter, I and my ministry faced a new challenge, but the difficulty was no hindrance to God; healings were confirmed everywhere, and people were being baptized in the Holy Spirit. I preached in churches, banquet halls, a night club, theaters, school auditoriums, and even a cafeteria. Most of Norway had never sat under a "word of knowledge" ministry like mine, nor had they ever heard "singing in the Spirit," which I call "the choir of angels." One newspaper headlined our meetings, "Mass Healings in Theatre."

On our last night in Oslo, Norway, we had a home service. Several prominent people came, among them the head priest of the Norway State Lutheran Church.

God performed Divine healings among those who were there. One lady who had had an infection for twenty-five years was healed after we had prayer together. Her doctor confirmed her healing in writing.

Our hosts were at the airport as we prepared to depart their country. The entire trip had been heart-warming and indicated to me that there was a whole wide world of wonderful people out there who would gladly welcome the full Gospel.

The day before our departure from Norway I bought a

birthday card for Valerie. It was printed in Norwegian. I contacted Valerie and told her that it was most important for her to meet my plane at Kennedy Airport.

As we came out the door from customs, I saw her standing with the wives of Simon Vikse and Clinton Utterback.

"I just want to say happy birthday," I said. "Close your eyes and give me your hand."

Everyone in our group started to sing happy birthday to her, and other passengers joined in the refrain. When Valerie felt the ring go on her finger, she gasped!

"You haven't changed your mind about marrying me, have you?" I asked.

"No . . . of course not," she said, still recovering from the surprise.

We kissed, and I laughed happily as she stared at my token of love. I had just twenty minutes before I would fly out to my next speaking engagement at PTL Club in Charlotte, North Carolina.

Tammy Bakker; Austin; and "Little People" friends, Dollie Warr and Margaret Orr, at the PTL Club in Charlotte, North Carolina.

Host David Maines with Austin on "100 Huntley Street," a syndicated Canadian TV program.

Host Joe Franklin and Austin listening to opera star Eleanor Steder on the "Joe Franklin Show," originating at WOR TV in New York.

# 33
# Dismissed

Knowing a proper legal "hearing" about me would be held in the near future, I decided to call members of the New York presbytery to see who would support me. I was stunned when one close friend said, "No, I cannot be your friend."

"But *you* of all people know about me and my ministry, and now you say that I can't count on you?"

"That's right," he retorted coldly. "I will go along with the brethren."

I slowly hung up the phone. I was too numb by now to feel anything.

Then I phoned Reverend Robert Rosen of Alcove, New York. He said, "I do not agree with them."

I had also ministered at his church, a little country church in the middle of nowhere. He should have been more easily intimidated by the presbytery than the rest, yet Reverend Rosen turned out to be a man of strength and integrity, and he was the only New York District minister to show any sympathy for me in my predicament.

I had a series of services scheduled in Missouri and was picked up at the St. Louis Airport by two youngsters in their teens. I marveled at their enthusiasm for God, hoping and praying that man would never succeed in dampening what they had in their hearts. "Thank you, Lord," I whispered silently, "for these Christian young people."

I met the pastor a few minutes before the main service. He was a big man with a round, kind face, and he extended what I felt was a sincere welcome.

That evening the church had one of its heaviest Sunday night crowds as word of the services had spread throughout the town. During the evening service I mentioned I would be there through Wednesday.

Following the service the pastor complimented me, then said, "You did make one mistake—the meetings are scheduled only through Tuesday, and you said Wednesday."

"That's the way we booked it," I answered. "I always go Sunday through Wednesday, or Sunday through Friday."

"Oh, no," said the pastor, "we always book it through Tuesday."

I was certain in my own mind that the original arrangement was through Wednesday, remembering correspondence to that effect.

I then shared with him the problems being caused by the New York presbytery. I mentioned that they were in session that very week, Monday through Wednesday.

The pastor stroked his chin. "Well, since this meeting was only scheduled through Tuesday," he suggested, "you could make the presbyters' meeting in New York on Wednesday this week!"

I began to understand the situation.

"I strongly suggest you take the first plane out tomorrow morning and attend that meeting," he advised.

I returned to my motel and dug into my suitcase. There were the two letters of confirmation and *both* stated that my engagement at the church was Sunday through Wednesday.

Then I called him. "Tell me, honestly, was there pressure upon you to cancel my last day?"

"I will only say," he replied rather sadly, "I, too, have had my problems with the hierarchy. You must go to that meeting. I frankly would like to see you stay in the church. Go and stand up for your rights and vindicate yourself. I will say this. I am going to be rebooking you into my church no matter what happens there."

I began my Wednesday at 5 A.M., flying from St. Louis to New York, dead tired from the strenuous, long lasting service the night before.

I made a hurried trip to my apartment, checked my answering service and found two calls, both labeled "emergency." The first was from Iowa. The pastor whose church I was scheduled to be at the following weekend was frantic. The New York District had informed him that I was "up on charges," painting a gruesome picture of wrong-doing without stating anything specific.

The other call on my service was from Don Richardson, secretary of the New York District. They were insisting I come immediately to face the presbytery and the charges now lodged against me. I called the Syracuse office and said I would be there within two hours.

I was angered by the fact that every church at which I was scheduled to speak had been contacted by the hierarchy. A feeling of outrage came over me as I thought about that pastor in Iowa. I felt a sense of bitterness, having given up everything to serve God and seeing the little I had left being destroyed. Yet a quiet feeling of calm began to settle over me as I walked through the doors of the New York District headquarters in Syracuse. The receptionist avoided looking me in the eye as I entered.

"I'll tell them you're here," she said and went upstairs. Some of the ministers were walking into the room. They hesitated, looked at me, then turned away.

I was beckoned to come forth. As I walked into the conference room, all the ministers who were gathered around the big table bolted to their feet, the rustling of the chairs scraping behind them in unison. One man walked toward me, extending his hand in friendship. It was Robert Rosen, true to his word.

I was motioned to the head of the table. Standing at the opposite end was Almon Bartholomew, the New York District superintendent.

"Brethren, be seated," he said, sustaining each word with melodious tones. "You, too, Brother Miles," he added.

Relieved that I was counted a "brother," I sat down.

"Brother Miles," Bartholomew continued, as though he were singing the words, "first of all . . . thank you for coming." The smile on his round face reached such a proportion that I watched in fascination in this dream-like setting, wondering how much further his mouth could stretch before breaking.

"I am grateful that . . . uh, the Lord allowed me to be here," I responded.

I looked at this gathering around the table. There was one whose eyes darted around, nervously wondering, it seemed to me, with whom to agree. Another looked pious enough to believe he was indeed sitting in judgment of an errant sinner. Still another seemed to have his mind everywhere but at the meeting.

I glanced at the others whose churches I had served. Their eyes dropped as I tried to make eye contact with them. One sat nervously. Another was leaning back on the two legs of his chair, hands folded in front of him, twirling his thumbs. I could visualize the legs breaking and the chair suddenly tipping all the way over. The balancing act continued throughout the hearing.

"Gentlemen," I addressed the group, "I want to make an opening statement. Until now, no official charges of wrongdoing have been brought against me. Yet, just this morning I spoke with another out of state pastor who had been contacted by *this* District. He was so disturbed by the malicious gossip he had heard from this district that he canceled my meeting!"

"Now, Brother Miles," sang Bartholomew, "unless you have written proof, all of this is hearsay, and you are wrongfully accusing the brethren."

"How about you, reverend?" I asked, pointing to Leon Cooke. "I understand that you told this presbytery at your last meeting that you 'know for a *fact*' that I have a second child. Well, my dear brother, that is erroneous!!!"

Bartholomew suddenly jumped from his chair. "Remember, Brother Miles," he scolded, "YOU are with men of God."

"Yes," I replied, "and with men of God there is always a Judas."

"Don't you call me a Judas," my old friend blurted out as he sprang to his feet.

"Thou hast said it," I replied evenly.

Bartholomew's jaw was now locked in a stern position, "Brother Miles, YOU are the one who is on trial here, not the

New York District." He waved to Don Richardson, who was operating the tape recorder, and said, "Strike that from the record." These erasures took place more than once!

After a lengthy discussion, Reverend Bartholomew said authoritatively, "Let's get down to the business at hand. Brother Miles, you are charged with refusing to give us any information regarding your first marriage. What do you have to say in your defense?"

"I was led to believe it was 'under the blood,' " I retorted. "Therefore, the subject is not open for discussion."

"Gentlemen," I continued, "if you have found no moral charges against me and since there has been no fault found with my doctrine or preaching, then why have you brought me up on charges to be dismissed when I was told I could resign?"

"Well, after all, Brother Miles," Bartholomew sang with a big smile, "you did have a previous marriage that ended in divorce."

I was infuriated by his attitude. I found reprehensible the idea of using a "Dismissal" as an instrument of punishment and ridicule—tantamount to a public flogging. Since the "Dismissed Ministers" names are circulated in the church bulletins, while the charges against them are not, the readers must rely on their imagination to conjure up the reason for the dismissal. Not even the so called "movie star gossip magazines" have the potential for hurt that a church "scandal sheet" has.

"You may think this is funny and be facetious about the matter," I said, "but I certainly do not appreciate your finding it so amusing!"

The smile suddenly vanished from his face as though concrete were being poured over him; the big grin became a scowl.

I continued my statement. "My first marriage was an event so painful it has put within me a hurt that will probably never be erased. You who are sitting here have no idea what that hurt is, and I would never wish such a thing on any one of you. The end of a marriage is a form of death, and one never fully recovers from it."

"We've quite well heard enough," Bartholomew interrupted, glaring at me. "It's time we vote upon your fitness as a minister and whether or not you should be dismissed from the fellowship."

I noticed the room seemed to be getting dark. One member of the presbytery automatically reached for the light switch. I glanced out the window. Dark clouds were gathering in the skies. There was a gentle rumble of thunder in the distance. The minister on my right looked at me, studied my face a moment, turned in his chair and looked out the window at the sky, then looked back at me. A strange expression came over his face. A breeze was stirring outside. A tremendous peace came over me.

"Before I leave this room so you can discuss this matter privately," I said, "I have just one more thing to say. I *will* continue to preach the Gospel. Yet, I *do* rebuke myself for not spending more time in prayer and for allowing anger to come into my heart."

Outside, the sky was getting darker, and the thunder was now coming right overhead. We could hear the wind whistle around the corner of the building.

"So I realize my own shortcomings. How I must grieve God by taking things of man too seriously. But even as the Apostle Paul said, "Who IS sufficient for these things." I must ask each of you who is sitting in judgment of me, can any one of you say that you are more qualified to preach the Gospel than I am?"

I noticed several moving nervously in their chairs, some dropping their eyes, others looking out the window at the angry sky. "Or, can you humbly admit that each of us has our shortcomings and that we should be praying for more unity instead of separation? Again, brethren, ask yourselves as I now ask you, WHO IS SUFFICIENT FOR THESE THINGS?"

"Why, none of us, Brother Miles, absolutely none of us," said the smiling face of Bartholomew in a deep entoning voice.

"Then, how can any of you sit in judgment of me to determine my fitness to preach?" I asked.

Outside, the sky was almost black with thunder and lightning. It started to rain. At one point the entire presbytery looked uneasily out the window as lightning struck something in the neighborhood.

"For all of our sakes—mine, yours, and the church—for the sake of the unsaved," I implored them, "just let me resign. A dismissal will invoke curiosity and questions that would be better left unanswered. Your decision will not prevent me from preaching the Gospel. The only thing you will decide is whether I am allowed to keep your particular union card. I will ask God to guide you in a wise decision."

I retired to the waiting room to await their decision. I was glad to see a coffee pot with some doughnuts. I hadn't eaten all day, having left St. Louis at 5 A.M. to attend this afternoon command performance. While sipping coffee, I opened a new book I had in my attache case called the *Archko Volume.*

Several minutes went by before Reverend Berg came out and said they were ready for me.

As I entered the room, the entire presbytery rose to their feet once again. Reverend Richardson, the district secretary, was the spokesman. He was youthful, almost owl-like behind his glasses. I remembered back to the time when I had spoken in a church he pastored in Utica, New York. His 700 seat church had been filled to capacity.

"Brother Miles," Reverend Richardson said, peering through his glasses, "here basically is our decision. Whereas: Austin Miles gave inaccurate information on his original application and had a previous wife, it has been unanimously voted to dismiss Austin Miles from the fellowship."

As I studied each of the men seated there, I was reminded of Psalm 35. "But in mine adversity they rejoiced, and gathered themselves together: yea, the abjects gathered themselves together against me . . .; they did tear me, and ceased not. . . . Yea, they opened their mouth wide against me, and said Aha, aha, our eye hath seen it."

I looked at my watch and rose following the pronouncement upon me.

"My dear brethren," I replied earnestly, "I have all

confidence that you truly felt you had a moral obligation to vote as you did."

What seemed to be a continuous roar of thunder shook the room; then, suddenly, all was quiet. The rain had stopped; the wind had stopped. Out of the corner of my eye I saw a ray coming in the window. Outside was a perfectly round rainbow in brilliant colors.

"As I mentioned before, gentlemen, I shall continue in the service of our Lord. I am leaving here to go to the Holy Land where I shall attempt to get my eyes off man and totally onto God." A long sigh preceded my next statement, "I shall pray for all of you."

"Oh, dear God, why?" I cried out in my anguish and despair as I slowly trudged to the car. My heart was breaking as I recalled the words of David from Psalms. "For it was not an enemy that reproached me: neither was it he that hateth me. . . . But it was thou, a man mine equal, my guide, and mine acquaintance. We took sweet counsel together, and walked unto the house of God in company. . . . Oh God, let them not say in their hearts, Ah, we have swallowed him up . . . we have put an end to him!"

# 34
# Israel

A leaf fluttered down from a tree on the Mount of Olives. I snatched it out of the air and put it in the Bible I was carrying. A Moslem man was moving his flock of sheep up the hill. Stretched out in the distance was the old city of Jerusalem. At last I was here. Joy flooded my heart, knowing I was in the place where Jesus had walked and talked. Earlier, I had received great comfort while praying in the Garden of Gethsemane, where I had enjoyed being alone and wandering about leisurely.

I walked to the spot where Jesus had fallen to his knees and wept for the city He loved so much:

> O Jerusalem, Jerusalem, thou that killest the prophets, and stonest them which are sent unto thee, how often would I have gathered thy children together, even as a hen gathereth her chickens under her wings, and ye would not. Behold, your house is left unto you desolate (Matt. 23:37-38).

I could understand why Jesus had wept. I knelt at that holy spot and silently prayed for understanding, forgiveness, and strength to continue my ministry.

In every holy spot, I asked God's blessing on my upcoming marriage to Val. We had not yet set a date as both of us wanted time to seek God's will for our lives.

Devoid of most material possessions since my divorce from Rose and having no immediate prospects for income, the idea of a wedding in the near future seemed highly unlikely. When Val said, "The only thing I want is for us to have matching wedding bands," I had jokingly replied, "They'll have to be cigar bands."

On the bank of the Jordan River, I lay back staring at the deep blue sky. Birds circled lazily overhead, occasionally dipping down to the water and then rising to play hide-and-seek with a cloud.

I thought again of Val's request for matching wedding bands. My mind drifted back to my twenty-first birthday when my mother had given me the first ring I had ever owned. Glancing down at my left hand, this ring brought back a flood of memories as my mother's face filled my consciousness.

Looking up, I saw the tour group coming about a block away. In a few minutes we would be taking part in a Jordan River baptism ceremony.

My right hand absent mindedly picked up a small stone, rolling it through my fingers. The stone clanked against the custom-made "fisherman" ring I wore on this hand. This exquisitely engraved work of art had been purchased by me in Texas shortly after my trip to the monastery. It represented the event of my spiritual commitment to Christ. Heaving a sigh, I realized that I didn't want to part with either one of these rings. I got up from the ground, dropping the stone, as the tour group approached.

The tour was being led by an Assemblies of God minister, and after our baptism in the Jordan, he asked me to speak at the site of the open tomb. The words poured directly from my heart—what I thought the open tomb meant to all of us gathered there.

As the group walked toward Golgotha, the minister slipped up beside me, put his arm around my shoulder, and said, "Brother Miles, there is one thing you should know. Not all of the brethren have deserted you."

By now we were standing at the foot of Calvary. "There's where it all happened," he said pointing up to the spot where Christ was crucified and rose from the dead. "That is where we were set free and given His protection."

We spent the night in a kibbutz, where I sought out the rabbi to discuss a matter which weighed heavily on my mind.

I had been treated as though I had committed an unpardonable sin because of my divorce. While the church held a divorced man unfit to preach the Gospel, the same churches would regularly have preaching from their pulpits "born-again" former drug addicts, murderers, thieves, child pornographers, prostitutes, etc.

Technically, I could, according to church doctrine, murder my wife, and, because I would then be single, be free to remarry in the church and even be ordained into the ministry. It just didn't make sense to me.

I asked the head rabbi his opinion on the ancient meanings in our Bible, specifically 1 Timothy 3:2, "A bishop then . . . must be the husband of one wife."

"When that was written," the rabbi told me, "there was vast polygamy in the land. This state of affairs was displeasing to God. That Scripture meant one wife at a time! If a wife should leave the husband, there is nothing in Scripture that says the bishop is bound to the first wife forever!"

The rabbi then pointed out 1 Corinthians 7:27-28, "Art thou bound unto a wife? seek not to be loosed. Art thou loosed from a wife? seek not a wife. But and if thou marry, thou hast not sinned. . . ."

I was able to meet with many Jewish scholars and students in Israel, giving me fascinating new insights into the Scriptures. As they shared with me about miracles they had personally witnessed, my own faith was greatly strengthened.

As our tour group stopped on the top of Mount Tabor at the scene of the transfiguration, I was again asked to speak. After the recitation from St. Matthew, I paused, then silently prayed again for Jesus to give me the strength to forgive those who had hurt me, to provide me with wisdom and guidance in my ministry, and to open a new door where Val and I would be welcomed to take the Gospel as a team. Prayerfully, I lifted my hands toward Heaven asking God to solve all my problems and believing that He could and would!

# 35
# The *Real* Ringmaster

"Praise God!" one person wrote in a letter to me. "The first thing I thought when I learned you had been dismissed was that you are no longer in denominational bondage."

It was true. I did feel a new sense of freedom unhindered by a denominational attachment. My spirits soared as I contemplated how I could continue to preach the Gospel and serve God effectively in His healing ministry. When an unexpected testimony arrived in the mail from Florida, I knew God still had His Hand on my life.

It was a confirmation of a cancer healing from L.A. Younger, a bank vice president from Palm Harbor. He had waited over eighteen months before writing to me just to make sure that his healing was real and had been confirmed by his doctors. Here was a man, who, by his own admission, had never heard of me or even believed.

His letter stated, "I felt like–O.K., get it over with and then leave me alone. . . . But in my hospital room . . . I felt a charge like electricity beginning at my neck and moving downward throughout my body. I really couldn't believe it. I cannot explain the sensation and still only know that it did happen–even to a *non believer!*"

His wife had asked me to visit him in the hospital after church services in Florida. I remembered how emaciated his cancer riddled body appeared and how my heart ached for him. It had been over a year and a half since I had seen or heard from him. God knew that I needed some form of encouragement for my ministry. This letter provided just the right amount and at the right time.

When an invitation came from the Aut Mori Grotto

Circus in Youngstown, Ohio, asking me to be the ringmaster for their annual benefit circus for handicapped children, I joyfully accepted the opportunity to re-create my old ringmaster role. I looked forward to seeing Pat Anthony, the lion trainer, and Ron and Joy Holiday, my dear old friends who were also booked on the show. It was a fantastic week of renewing acquaintances mixed in with a demanding and hectic schedule.

The PTL Club camera crews came to film the event and a circus *first!* I would be holding a church service in the "Center Ring." The public had been invited to join the circus personnel for services after the performance.

The kneeling altar that had been put in my dressing room was brought into the center ring; then all the lights were darkened, except for two spotlights. I remained in my ringmaster's costume and gave my testimony. After all, my ministry began in the circus when I was dressed in the red tails. During the service the lions began to roar. "Now that is beautiful music," I said. "They belong here; they are as much a part of the circus as all of us. And God belongs here, as He does with all people."

Many of the performers had slipped into the arena in their street clothes, sitting anonymously in the dark, watching and listening. At the end of the service people thronged to the center ring. One performer told me that he had not been to a place of worship since he came to this country from Germany many years ago. Ron Holiday said simply, "This, tonight, was church."

On Easter Sunday, 1978, I ordained Samuel Siligato as a "minister" of the First Charismatic Church. It seemed the proper time for the beautiful dedication. On the day that Christ rose from the dead, a young man was being raised up for the ministry. The ceremony was held at the PTL Club Heritage Village Church as part of the Easter service.

Several months later a surprise and most welcomed call came from Windsor, Ontario. John and Hilda Mahoney of the Fountain Restaurant had seen me on a television program hosted by a minister in Detroit. They asked if I could come to Canada for a week to preach the Gospel in one of their banquet rooms.

Three of us traveled to Canada, by car—Valerie's mother Grace, a dear friend named John Earl, and myself.

On Friday, May 19, 1978, two hours prior to the evening services on our last day at the "Fountain," Valerie telephoned from New Jersey. She had finally picked a date for us to be married; "Next Thursday, May 25," she said excitedly. "We can have the ceremony and reception at my grandmother's house in Cape May by the ocean. I've checked with the rest of the family, and it's a good time for everyone. What do you think?"

"That's great, Val," I answered. "We should arrive back home Monday."

Secretly I was concerned. I still had no money for a ring and no immediate prospects for employment. Both of my rings symbolized occasions so special to me that I didn't want to wear another; yet, I knew Valerie would be very disappointed if we didn't have matching wedding bands.

"I honestly don't know what to do," I confided to Grace and John Earl after her phone call.

Two hours later the last of our Canadian services began. The Spirit moved in a marvelous way as the Lord poured out many blessings. A multitude of people stayed, and I was faced with a three hour prayer line.

As the people moved steadily and slowly toward me, a young Canadian man came forward and thrust an object wrapped in tissue paper into my hand, then sank to the floor overwhelmed as the Holy Spirit touched him. I placed the object in my pocket and moved to pray for another. Meanwhile, the young man had risen and disappeared into the crowd.

After the service, when the lights were brightened, I reached into my pocket for the object I had placed there. Astonished, I held it up to the light for Grace, John, and the Mahoneys to see.

"I just can't believe it,'' Grace exclaimed. "It's an exact duplicate of your 'fisherman's' ring!"

My heart was pounding wildly. Unbelievable, but true! God had blessed us with a miracle and an answer to my dilemma with an exact mate to my "fisherman" ring.

It was a festive occasion at Grandma and Grandpa Thomas's house. Sammy performed the ceremony, his first. He was especially handsome in an elegant three piece white suit and shoes with black vestment and clerical collar. We chose to be married out in the backyard by a little wishing well. There, we would be under God's ceiling. Stretched out before us was the ocean.

As beautiful and solemn as the occasion was, when Sammy asked us to vow our worldly goods to one another, we both grinned as we looked down at the wedding ring God had provided. The biblical verse, "Seek ye first the kingdom of God . . . and all these things shall be added unto you," flashed through my mind.

Then, Valerie and I knelt for an additional vow as Sammy anointed us with oil, stating that not only was this a union of two people as man and wife but also a uniting together to serve God as His ministers. The overflowing joy and contentment I felt at this time could only adequately be described as "the Peace that passeth all understanding."

After the ceremony Grace's Aunt Catherine detected something unusual in the Polaroid photos which were taken throughout the ceremony. "Look!" she exclaimed. "There is a perfect cross next to you in every picture."

Sure enough, God once again had made His presence known.

After the guests were gone, Valerie and I walked across the street, looking out over the ocean. We held hands as we strolled toward the water.

"Honey," I said, "I am going to know for the first time how beautiful a loving and spiritual relationship can be."

By now we both had kicked off our shoes, tossed them over our shoulders, and continued our walk just near the water's edge. "I was just thinking," I continued. "Not only has God been meeting our needs, but something else—I never did have brothers and sisters or grandparents. Now God has given me a whole new family. He has given me things I never had before."

Squeezing Val's hand in mine, I said, "I'm so happy."

The sun had begun to dip down, casting a golden

glow over the water and horizon.

"You know, Val," I said, as we watched the sun disappear, ending another day, "when we give our lives over totally to Christ, He is able to take wrecks and turn them to rocks. It is only then that we are able to build a solid work for Him."

"I know," Val whispered softly. "I can never hope to repay Jesus for what He did for me. I am not just living; I'm alive!"

> For we know that all things work together for good to them that love God, to them who are called according to his purpose (Romans 8:28).

# Epilogue

Not by might, nor by power, but by my spirit saith the LORD of hosts" (Zech. 4:6).

Within a year the "angel unaware" who had supplied the wedding ring identified himself during another Canadian service as Ron Backmeier, 479 McKuen, Windsor, Ontario.

Ruth Sebastiano (chapter thirty-two) walked through the doors of the PTL Club to share her testimony with the world.

On a national telecast in Canada–100 Huntley St., with David Maines–Austin was given a "word of knowledge" that resulted in confirmed healings throughout the area.

Three other nationwide TV programs requested interviews.

*Voice,* the International Full Gospel Businessmen's magazine, featured Austin in a surprise article in the October, 1979, issue.

Two other international magazines followed with more coverage.

Doors immediately opened wide to the Methodist, Presbyterian, Church of God, many independent churches, and to Assemblies of God churches as God's Holy Spirit paved the way for a new ministry that spanned many denominations and two countries.

October 1979. . . . An accomplice of David Berkowitz, the New York killer dubbed "Son of Sam" was caught in Minot, North Dakota. The accomplice admitted that both he and David Berkowitz had been involved in and practiced "devil worship" rites.

> For we wrestle not against flesh and blood, but against principalities, against powers, against the rulers of the darkness of this world, against spiritual wickedness in high places (of authority)" (Eph. 6:12).